A COURSE IN MIRACLES
AND
CHRISTIANITY

A Dialogue

WITHDRAWN

A COURSE IN MIRACLES
AND
CHRISTIANITY

A Dialogue

Kenneth Wapnick, Ph.D.
W. Norris Clarke, S.J., Ph.D.

Foundation for *A Course in Miracles*

Foundation for *A Course in Miracles*
1275 Tennanah Lake Road
Roscoe, NY 12776-5905

Copyright 1995 by the
Foundation for *A Course in Miracles*

Printed in the United States of America

Portions of *A Course in Miracles*® copyright 1975, 1992, reprinted by permission of the Foundation for Inner Peace.

A Course in Miracles is a registered service mark and trademark of the Foundation for Inner Peace. Used by permission.

Library of Congress Cataloging in Publication Data

Wapnick, Kenneth–
    A Course in miracles and Christianity : a dialogue / Kenneth Wapnick, W. Norris Clarke.
        ISBN 0-933291-18-3
    1. Course in miracles. 2. Christianity. I. Clarke, W. Norris, (William Norris)–. II. Title.
    BP605.C68W3585 1994
    299'.93--dc20
                                                        94-10394

CONTENTS

Preface

Kenneth Wapnick

On January 4, 1989 at the Foundation for *A Course in Miracles*, I engaged in a dialogue with Father W. Norris Clarke, a Roman Catholic Jesuit priest and philosopher, on the differences and similarities between *A Course in Miracles* and traditional or biblical Christianity. Fr. Clarke is an unusual priest and Catholic philosopher, insofar as he has an open-minded and non-judgmental approach to non–Catholic teachings, all the while retaining his very strong personal faith in the truth of the Roman Catholic Church. His background is impressive, and is summarized briefly here:

Rev. W. Norris Clarke, S.J., earned his Ph.D. at the University of Louvain, and was Professor of Philosophy at Fordham University in New York for thirty-one years until his retirement in 1985. Since his retirement, he has been a visiting professor at universities and colleges across the nation. He founded, and for twenty-five years was Editor-in-Chief of the *International Philosophical Quarterly*. He has served as President of both the American Catholic Philosophical Association and the Metaphysical Society of America, and as a member of the Executive Council of the American Philosophical Association. He has lectured widely, and has published more than sixty articles in philosophical and theological journals and anthologies, and has authored three books. He is loved and respected in religious and philosophical circles around the world as a man of deep faith and wisdom.

Numerous awards and honors have been bestowed on Fr. Clarke in recognition of his outstanding qualities as a teacher, a philosopher, and a priest. Among these honors are the American Catholic Philosophical Association's Aquinas

Medal for distinguished contribution to Christian philosophy, the Outstanding Teacher Award from Fordham University, and Honorary Doctoral Degrees from Villanova University and Wheeling Jesuit College. I am honored that he accepted the Foundation's invitation to join me in this dialogue.

Fr. Clarke and I have been friends for many years, and he was the ideal person with whom to enter into this dialogue. Our conversation was video-taped, but unfortunately the quality of the tapes was unsatisfactory. This book is an edited version of the dialogue, which includes minor changes made to enhance readability, and additional clarifying material with appropriate references to *A Course in Miracles*[1] and the Bible. I have added a special introduction for this book, an appendix that introduces *A Course in Miracles* to the reader unfamiliar with it, and a glossary of many of the terms and names that are referred to throughout the dialogue for those who may not know them.

I am extremely grateful to Fr. Clarke for his willingness to participate so graciously in this dialogue, and for the clarity he has brought to the issue of comparing *A Course in Miracles* and biblical Christianity. I also wish to thank my wife Gloria and Rosemarie LoSasso, the Foundation's Director of Publications (originally Fr. Clarke's doctoral student at Fordham University)—both of whom were present during the dialogue—for their many suggestions in preparation for the dialogue itself, as well as for this book.

---

1. These references are cited in two ways: page numbers are given for the first edition; the full citation is given for the numbering system in the second edition.

INTRODUCTION

Kenneth Wapnick

For approximately 2,000 years, the Bible has had an incredible hold on Western civilization, and has clearly dominated all other forms of religious thought. Moreover, it has exerted the most powerful influence over the course of Western political, economic, social, moral, and artistic history. The reason for such a hold, when one examines the Bible from the perspective of *A Course in Miracles*, is the clear expression its theology gives to the ego thought system, justifying for its believers their own needs to be special. (By the same token, biblical believers would draw similar conclusions about the Course's current popularity.) Incidentally, for the purposes of this dialogue, the focus was more on the New Testament, although as the discussion will show, the Old and New Testaments together reflect a common theological orientation.

Many students of *A Course in Miracles* have been tempted to call the Course the "Third Testament," expressing their belief that it represents the same basic theology of the Bible, although in a more "purified" (i.e., less ego-dominated) or more spiritually evolved form. As will be clear from the dialogue between Fr. Clarke and me, this grossly distorts what *A Course in Miracles* teaches, and is a real disservice to both the Course and the Bible. In fact, the Course and the Bible reflect *entirely different* and *mutually exclusive theologies* that can never be integrated into one coherent spirituality.

This crucial difference can be summarized in the statement that for Christians the Bible is *the* Word of God (Christians differing only to the degree of literalness the various Churches ascribe to it), while from the perspective of *A Course in Miracles*, the Bible would be seen as just one among many religious documents that reflect the consciousness of the time and culture in which they were written. Based upon the important distinction the Course draws between form and content, the Bible would be understood as merely the *form* in which a people expressed its view of the world and of God, no different therefore from the works of the great Western poets such as Homer, the Greek tragedians, Dante, Shakespeare, and Goethe, among countless other poets and artists.

The shared *content* of all inspired works is the desire to express what is true for their authors, regardless of the form of artistic expression in which it comes. Understood from this point of view, Christianity's mistake has been to elevate the Bible's historical and theological statements into absolute truths, no different from a lover of Shakespeare asserting that his great history plays render an accurate account of English history.

Therefore, to attempt such a reconciliation between these two spiritual paths—A *Course in Miracles* and traditional Christianity—must inevitably lead to frustration at best, and severe distortion at worst. Indeed, Fr. Clarke has commented, as I mention at the end of the dialogue, that to speak of the Course as a "correction" for Christianity (as I myself had occasionally spoken of it in the past) is misleading. To correct something implies that you are still retaining the basic framework of what you are correcting. A *Course in Miracles*, on the other hand, directly refutes the very basis of the Christian faith, leaving nothing on which Christians can base their beliefs. Succinctly stated, here are some of the major differences between the two:

1) A *Course in Miracles* teaches that God did not create the physical universe, which includes all matter, form, and the body; the Bible states that He did.

2) The God of A *Course in Miracles* does not even know about the sin of separation (since to know about it would

make it real), let alone react to it; the God of the Bible perceives sin directly, as is portrayed in the Garden of Eden story discussed later in the dialogue, and His responses to it are vigorous, dramatic, and at times punitive, to say the very least.

3) *A Course in Miracles'* Jesus is equal to everyone else, a part of God's one Son or Christ; the Bible's Jesus is seen as special, apart, and therefore ontologically different from everyone else, being God's only begotten Son, the second person of the Trinity.

4) The Jesus of *A Course in Miracles* is not sent by God to suffer and die on the cross in a sacrificial act of atonement for sin, but rather teaches that there is no sin by demonstrating that nothing happened to him in reality, for sin has no effect on the Love of God; the Jesus of the Bible agonizes, suffers, and dies for the sins of the world in an act that brings vicarious salvation to humanity, thereby establishing sin and death as real, and moreover clearly reflecting that God has been affected by Adam's sin and must respond to its actual presence in the world by sacrificing His beloved Son.

Thus, from the perspective of *A Course in Miracles*, the God of the Bible, Creator of the world and author of the atonement plan of suffering, sacrifice, and death, is an ego God. He is one Who clearly represents the thought system of the ego's specialness that the Course sets forth. Jesus himself makes these parallels in the text, as seen in the opening sections in Chapters 3 and 6, the Introduction to Chapter 13, the important section in Chapter 23, "The Laws of Chaos," as well as in many, many other places in the Course.

In summary, therefore, we can conclude that there is no way one can reconcile the God or theology of the Bible with the theology found in *A Course in Miracles*. Moreover, the figure of Jesus in the Bible is totally incompatible with the Jesus who authored *A Course in Miracles*. In fact, Jesus himself states in the Course, in obvious reference to the historical images that were drawn from the biblical ones, that bitter idols were made of him "who would be only brother to the world" (manual, p. 86; C-5.5:7). It is a continual source of amazement—given the clear distinctions between the biblical and Course figures—for one to observe how frequently this reconciliation is attempted. In fact, Fr. Clarke makes this observation in the course of the dialogue.

I have frequently made the public comment that one of the most important lessons a student of *A Course in Miracles* can learn is how to disagree with someone (whether that person be on another spiritual path, or a student of the Course) without it being an attack. In our world of multiplicity, where personal projections and perceptions rule, it is almost impossible for people to agree when it comes to systems of thought, or on almost anything else for that matter. My father in fact used to say about people holding differences of opinion: "That's what makes horse races." It is also what makes the ego's universe, reflecting the original ego thought that the Son is separate and different in kind from his Creator. Jesus himself comments in *A Course in Miracles*, as I quote below in the dialogue: "A universal theology is impossible, but a universal experience is not only possible but necessary" (manual, p. 73; C-in.2:5). The universal experience is love, and the dialogue with Fr. Clarke was held in the loving spirit of respecting differences, agreeing to disagree as it were, thus offering an example of differing without judgment or attack.

Therefore, it is our hope that this book will contribute to a better understanding of the thought systems of *A Course in Miracles* and biblical Christianity. It was neither Fr. Clarke's nor my purpose to *debate* the clear differences which I identified briefly above, and will be discussed more fully in the dialogue. Rather, our purpose was to state them simply, defining the differences (and similarities where they occur) as clearly as possible.

A Course in Miracles, in fact, itself teaches through the use of contrasts, as it frequently states (e.g., text, pp. 249, 252; T-13.XI.6:1-3; T-14.II.1:2-3), even though such differences are absent in Heaven, the state of perfect oneness and undifferentiated unity. At our level of learning, however, where we believe we exist within the ego thought system of time and space, of separation and specialness, we are still in need of contrast to learn the Holy Spirit's lessons of forgiveness instead of the ego's lessons of attack. Indeed, one of the principal contrasts Jesus uses in the Course to present his thought system is with traditional Christianity, with an occasional specific reference to Roman Catholicism. Thus in *A Course in Miracles'* presentation itself, Jesus shows us that differences can be acknowledged in a loving way, in a spirit of non-opposition and without confrontation, and lovingly serving a pedagogical purpose.

Therefore, the spirit in which this dialogue has been entered is also meant to reflect the Course's view of itself: that it is only one among many thousands of spiritual paths (manual, p. 3; M-1.4:1-2). For in the end, it is the non-judgmental experience of our oneness with God and His creation, rather than the mere acceptance of *A Course in Miracles'* theology as opposed to that of another spiritual system, that constitutes the aim of the Course's curriculum.

The dialogue has been divided into an Introduction, and five chapters: The Origin of the World, Jesus, The Eucharist, Living in the World, and Summary and Conclusions.

One final point: *A Course in Miracles* has its own rules of capitalization which have been followed in my part of the dialogue—e.g., all nouns and pronouns related to God, Christ, and the Holy Spirit are capitalized; the "Son of God," a term which includes all children of God, is also capitalized. Fr. Clarke's preferred system of capitalization has been followed in his.

THE DIALOGUE

INTRODUCTION

CLARKE: I would like to begin this conversation with expressing my appreciation of Dr. Wapnick's—I am going to call him Kenneth from now on—willingness to air the common differences between traditional Christianity, and *A Course in Miracles*.

A few years ago when I first heard about *A Course in Miracles*, I took a six-hour workshop with Kenneth on the basic doctrine of the Course. It seemed clear to me that there were a number of incompatibilities between Christianity and *A Course in Miracles*, and to my surprise, he was entirely willing to admit that. I really respect that authenticity. He is not trying to fudge the differences. He admits quite clearly that there are serious differences and incompatibilities between the Course and traditional Christianity, particularly as expressed in Roman Catholicism, but also, I think, in most of the main-line Protestant traditions, too. He admits that, and is not trying to conceal it. That is admirable, because a few of the people who present *A Course in Miracles* do try to fudge, it seems to me, and say that the Course is just an extension of ordinary Christian teachings. Kenneth clearly repudiates that, and in so doing shows himself a truly authentic, honest teacher seeking to present the Course on its own merits as a path in its own way—which is fine if people want to follow that path, as long as they know what they are doing.

WAPNICK: If I may return the compliment, in addition to having great admiration for Fr. Norris Clarke as a philosopher and as a teacher, I also have great admiration and respect for the gentleness and defenselessness with which he very clearly presents these differences and the position of the Bible and traditional Christianity; and it is because of this that we are particularly grateful to have you here with us, Norris, to do this dialogue together.

I think as a beginning, what might help clarify some of the differences and similarities we will be talking about is to highlight the fact that *A Course in Miracles* is basically written on two levels. The first of these, which I sometimes call Level One, is the metaphysical level, which contrasts the pure state of Heaven as the only reality and the only truth with the illusory nature of the physical world. So this metaphysical level contrasts Heaven and the world, God and the ego, truth and illusion.

The second level that the Course is written on is what I sometimes also call Level Two, which is the more practical level of the Course's teachings on forgiveness. On this level, *A Course in Miracles* deals only with this physical world and our experiences here as a dream, and basically contrasts two ways of perceiving this world and living in this world: the first is following the guidance of the Holy Spirit; the second is listening to the voice of the ego. The Holy Spirit's Voice speaks of unity, joining, and forgiveness, while the ego's voice speaks of sin, guilt, fear, separation, attack, and judgment. It is within these two levels that we will attempt to explore some of the similarities, as well as the major and important differences between *A Course in Miracles* and traditional Christianity.

CLARKE: I do have my difficulties with the notion of two different levels, not so much of reality but of being real and unreal, illusion and reality, but we might get into that later.

WAPNICK: We probably will.

THE ORIGIN OF THE WORLD

CLARKE: The first and most fundamental point of difference between Christianity and the Course is the first article of the Creed[2] or declaration of Christian belief recited every Sunday in churches around the world: "I believe in one God, the Father Almighty, Creator of heaven and earth, of all that is seen and unseen." This means that everything real that is not God is brought into being out of nothing (i.e., out of no preexisting material) by God alone. The Course explicitly denies this, saying that God himself is not only not responsible for creating the material world, but in fact does not even know of its existence, since it is not actually real. It is really only a dream state, thought up by a fragment of the divine or Christ consciousness that broke off from the pure divine consciousness and spun out this dream world as an act of independence from God and a refuge for the ego turning away in flight from God.

In the Book of Genesis in the Old Testament, or Jewish part of the Bible, accepted by Christians, too, as part of their faith, it says that God made the earth and all the living things on it, and finally human beings, and "saw that it was all *very good*." This basic goodness of the material world, despite all its imperfections, is central to Christian belief, so that the final state of blessedness of the saved in heaven, including the state of Jesus Christ, will be one of a risen and glorified body, not a rejection of matter but a lifting it up into the life of spirit.

Thus, Christian faith could not accept that anything other than God himself could have created this or any finite world out of nothing, let alone its having occurred contrary to, or unknown to, the will of God. Nor could it accept that this finite material world is not a real world but only a dream

---

2. See the Appendix, p. 101, for the full text of the Nicene Creed.

11

world or a world purely of thought, of ideas only. For, first of all, this world is the theater of all our moral activity and hence free decisions, the necessary path for us to walk in order to be admitted into our final blessedness with God in heaven; and free moral decisions can be made only by real persons with real wills, not by ideas or dream-persons. Second, the firm reality of this material world is backed up by the fact that God himself in his Son Jesus took on a real human body from a real human mother, Mary, and has risen from the dead in this same real body, now eternally existing in heaven, and we, too, are destined to rise again in our own real (though profoundly changed and spiritualized) bodies. Furthermore, new babies born into this world are truly new persons entering into the Kingdom of God, with the spirit of life truly breathed into them by God, who grow up slowly to be responsible moral persons. They are not merely dream productions or unreal projections of ideas, or fragments breaking off from a dreaming consciousness (consciously or unconsciously), but real persons with the power of free moral decision.

WAPNICK: If I may, Norris, I should like to comment on your statements and amplify the differences between *A Course in Miracles* and traditional Christianity.

To begin with, the Course would certainly not see the world as being good, because it states that "the world was made as an attack on God" (workbook, p. 403; W-pII.3.2:1). Having come into existence as a result of the projection of the mind's thought of attack and separation from God, the world must then mirror the horror of this thought of having destroyed God and Heaven. And it is this thought of separation that is the Course's definition of sin. Thus the only "good" thing about the world is that it can serve as our classroom in which we learn the Holy Spirit's lessons of forgiveness, which I will elaborate on later. But in and of itself the world has nothing redeeming about it.

Second, you mentioned the idea about "the saved in Heaven," which clearly implies that there are some who are "unsaved." This could never be the case according to *A Course in Miracles*, since the Sonship of God is understood as being perfectly united and at one with itself and with its Creator. And so in reality there could be no such distinctions as "good" and "bad," or "saved" and "unsaved." Only in a dualistic dream could such distinctions seem to occur. The implication of such a division, moreover, is that part of what God created perfect can choose, because of "free will," to will against Him. As a result, that part must suffer the consequences of God's condemnation up to and including eternal damnation. All of this, again, would be impossible in the Course's concept of the perfect oneness of God's Love.

I should also like to comment briefly on the word "consciousness." The Course's understanding of "consciousness" is that it is the domain of the ego, "the first split introduced into the mind after the separation" (text, p. 37; T-3.IV.2:1). The word "consciousness" thus implies a duality: there is someone who observes and something that is observed. I am conscious of something; I am thinking of something. And so the state that you are describing, Norris— "divine consciousness"—would really be one of undifferentiated unity, formlessness in the Course's understanding, since it reserves use of the word "consciousness" for the dualistic world of perception and thought, in distinction from how many people are currently using the word, and as you did, Norris. Thus, I am speaking of it here only as existing in the ego's thought system, because, again, it implies a duality, what *A Course in Miracles* refers to as the world of perception and illusion. I understand, though, that you may want to continue to use the term in accordance with your framework.

With regard to the two contrasting attitudes toward the world, I would agree with you totally, except in one regard. I will go back to the origin, because I believe that that is a crucial difference. What makes *A Course in Miracles* different and unique among world spiritualities, which is why I talk about a Level One and a Level Two, is that on the one hand the Course teaches that this world and the body were not created by God, and in fact says at one point, as I stated previously, that this "world was made as an attack on God"—which accentuates the radicalness of the Course's position even more. On the other hand, however, the Course does not foster an attitude in its students of denigrating the world, but rather, as I have just said, an attitude of seeing the world as a classroom, in which the Holy Spirit teaches us the lessons of forgiveness that lead us back to God.

So while there would be a crucial difference in terms of the cosmogony of the world—the origin of the world—the attitude that *A Course in Miracles* would foster in its students would not be one of hatred of the world, as some Gnostics experienced for example. Rather it would be a feeling of gratitude that God did not create this nightmare dream we call the world, which means that it is inherently unreal. Therefore, a student of *A Course in Miracles* would also be grateful for the opportunity to accept the correction of forgiveness that our teacher Jesus offers to us.

Marcion, a second-century Gnostic teacher, talked about the world as being a "puny cell" in the mind of its creator—namely, the ego. *A Course in Miracles* would definitely not agree with that kind of attitude, nor of course would Christianity. But certainly in terms of the origin and nature of the world, as stated in the Creed, there is unquestionably a clear difference between the position that the Course takes and that of biblical Christianity. The important issue of morality and free will which you raised, Norris, I'll come back to later in our discussion.

CLARKE: I agree that the Course does not assert that this material world is evil, which makes it different from the other Gnostic doctrines around the time of early Christianity that are in many ways similar to it, and which the Christian

Churches always strongly opposed as quite contrary to the spirit and letter of Christianity. Thus the Course teaches that this world is, for those in it, a positive school for learning how to wake up and return to our true real state of perfect union with God. But this material world of differentiated persons is still only a dream world, not a truly real world of genuinely distinct, real persons. This a Christian believer would not find possible to accept; for him this world is also a "classroom" for awakening to our true nature and personal moral and religious development, but this can only be done by real moral individuals in a real world confronting them with real free decisions. Thus the key similarity with the ancient Gnostic doctrines still remains, that this material world of many distinct persons is not the work of God, and not real and good in itself.

There also seems to be here a profound echo of another great ancient doctrine, that of the Hindu Advaita (or nondualistic) Vedanta, according to which the Ultimate Reality, or Brahman, is all that truly is, "One without a second," and all else that seems to those in ignorance to be real is in fact an illusion, a product of dream consciousness or *maya*. I think you yourself, Kenneth, have somewhere admitted these affinities with both Gnosticism and Advaita Vedanta. But for the Christian there are only two options open: either this world is not genuinely real, and then it cannot be the field for genuine moral development and response to God as the path to final union with him; or it is a truly real world, and then only God could create it out of nothing. I'll come back to this presently. Despite all its imperfections, this world does manifest the latter by its extraordinarily rich and interlocking order and immense energy.

WAPNICK: Yes, I think your point about the world or cosmos being such an impressive achievement reflects your love of Plato, who obviously would make the same point. While I think there are many things the Course has in common with

Platonism and Neoplatonism, that would not be among them, certainly. A *Course in Miracles* would say that the order and logic that exist in the world or cosmos is an *apparent* order—born of the ego—because it is a world of form and change. Therefore, the world is really in *dis*order because it is the denial of the formlessness and changelessness of God. In fact, in a section called "The Laws of Chaos," the Course distinctly sets forth the non-logical and insane premises of the world, beginning with the first law of chaos that there is a hierarchy of illusions and that truth is relative and not absolute. Thus, according to this ego principle, certain things or people in this world would be more valuable, important, or holy than others.

Therefore, that *lack* of true order and *presence* of insane chaos would be the proof that the physical universe could not have been created by God, but rather that it came from the fevered miscreations of the ego mind, which is inherently disordered because of its dualistic and separated nature. Truth, in *A Course in Miracles*, is non-dualistic and so must be absolute and not relative, the exact opposite of the state of the split mind.

CLARKE: It would have to be a pretty powerful mind.

WAPNICK: Yes, A *Course in Miracles* does say that. I think we both would agree that our minds are powerful. What the Course would say, in fact, what it does say in different ways, is that one of the purposes the ego had in making up this world—the home of this false self of ours—was to have an opposite to Heaven; in effect, to try to out-do God, to behold the seeming majesty of the cosmos and say to God, on an unconscious level, obviously: "Look what I have done! I can create as First Cause and do something as good, if not better, than You!" This clearly reflects the arrogance of the ego. Furthermore, the ego boasts it can make a world which, as the opposite of Heaven, ends up as its substitute.

CLARKE: I see. But that ego certainly would not be our own ego...

WAPNICK: Not the individualized ego that we would identify as Kenneth's or Norris.' The Course describes a process of fragmentation which occurred when the Son of God *seemed* to fall asleep, which I know is a point you have difficulty with, and which we will come back to. Originally, the separation began when one mind fragmented, similar to the process of cellular mitosis, and just kept fragmenting over and over and over again, subdividing over and over, the end product of which is this world of multiplicity and separated selves. But in reality, we are all part of one self: both one false self, the ego self, as well as one collective Self, which *A Course in Miracles* calls Christ, our spiritual Identity.

CLARKE: That is a very helpful and illuminating summary of the Course's main position about the origins of what we call "our world," or our present situation. But this brings out even more clearly the basic differences between the Course and traditional Christianity. In terms of the doctrine of God alone as the Creator of all that is, out of nothing, there are only two options open to the Christian: 1) Either this material world in which we seem to live is in some way, to some degree, *real*—and in this case it could not be produced out of nothing by any being other than God himself—it could not be produced by any real mind somehow broken off from the one divine mind, unknown to this divine mind, let alone contrary to the divine will; 2) or else this "world" in which we are at present operating is only a world of pure thoughts, ideas, with no reality beyond that of mere ideas, images. Then it could not be the theater for real moral decisions, for deciding to turn back to God, to turn away from illusion—such a decision cannot be itself only an illusion—nor for doing such profoundly good actions as leading a life of forgiveness and love, of which the Course speaks so beautifully on its second or practical level. It is not clear how a dream classroom can really be a classroom for teaching individual wills to make the individual real decisions—or refuse to do so—to turn back to God. It does not seem that merely dream or idea-characters can make real significant individual moral decisions, unless in some meaning of dream or thought that is far more powerful and "real" than what we ordinarily mean by it in our languages, and so fall back under the first option rejected above.

I think we would have similar difficulty in rendering meaningful the process described by the Course as a progressive fragmentation of egos from one larger original one, namely: would this be a real fragmentation? How could only imaginary egos make real moral decisions, good or bad? Would they just fragment in an unconscious, quasi-biological process or by deliberate, spiritual choice of the central ego? I guess the main difficulty here is how significant moral decisions could be made by only unreal imaginary, dream characters. In a word, the second practical level of the Course's teaching, with all its rich psychological and spiritual wisdom and exhortations to disciplined living, seems to be a much more real and existentially dramatic one than allowed by the first level theory of the Course. That is what really leaves a Christian so puzzled: how such a real/dream world could ever have gotten started in the first place completely unknown to and independent of God, sole Creator of all that is real in any way, or how the Creator could not know what many of his own creatures know—this dramatic dream world of moral decisions which they know and live in. There you have, simply put, why a traditional Christian believer in God as Creator of all that is could not accept the Course taken literally as it is.

WAPNICK: Of course not, anymore than a student of *A Course in Miracles* could accept the traditional Christian view. As we have already stated, and will no doubt state again, *A Course in Miracles* and the Bible reflect mutually exclusive spiritual paths.

I'll respond to your last point later; but first some additional comments about the nature of the dream: The Course's central metaphysical teaching is that the world of perception and form—what the Hindus refer to as the world of multiplicity—is totally illusory, and is simply a dream in which the Son of God believed he could separate from his Creator and Source, and make a world and self that is the opposite of Heaven. It is no different—in fact, the analogy is drawn several times in the Course—from our experience at night while we dream. As long as we are asleep, the images we "see" appear very real to us: the people we interact with, the places we are in, the sounds, tastes, and tactile stimulation that are part of the dream—all these are experienced as quite real to us while we are asleep and dreaming. And this includes the dream happenings that "break" the usual laws of time and space. It is only when we awaken from the dream that we become aware that none of what had seemed so tangible and real has really occurred at all. Throughout all the events of the dream, we remained safely asleep in our bed.

What is referred to in *A Course in Miracles* as our waking dreams—what we think of as our real lives—are no different: same content, different form. Thus, we only *think* we are here, experiencing ourselves as living in a world that was created outside ourselves, existing autonomously and independently of our minds. But in truth, all this is a collective dream, in which all of the figures—animate and inanimate, regardless of where each falls within what is sometimes called the great chain of being—are equally illusory, just as in a sleeping dream. It is a dream of cosmic proportions, almost inconceivable in its vastness. And yet it remains, after all, simply a dream, outside the mind of God, the only Reality.

I'll return to some of your other points about morality and decisions later in the dialogue, Norris, but suffice it to say, once again, there is no way that a biblical Christian and a student of *A Course in Miracles* could ever find mutual grounds of agreement when it comes to questions of theology or cosmology.

CLARKE: Before we leave this topic of creation, I think it is only fair to say something about the different ways in which each position views the *problem of evil*. For the difficulty of reconciling the obvious evil in this present world of ours with the notion of creation by a good God is one of the main objections of the Course against this central belief of traditional Christianity. As you said earlier, the Course considers the so-called order of this world as really an insane kind of order, with all of its imperfections, diseases, disasters of all kinds, and especially the fierce competition of one species living by devouring others, which is the law throughout the subhuman living world. If God is going to create any world, it must be one that resembles the divine perfections, not one filled with evil.

Let us be perfectly honest. The problem of evil is indeed one filled with mystery for our limited human minds, and not one possible for us to crack and completely comprehend with our own limited vision of world history and what God is planning for beyond death. But Christian faith can shed considerable light on it, I think. First, the moral evils of the world, deriving from the free evil moral decisions of human beings and their consequences, such as hatred, selfishness, exploiting of others, etc., are our own responsibility and not due to God at all, who only permits this so as not to override our freedom and remove our possibilities of doing moral good, too. Freely given love and service by human beings is such a lofty good that God is willing to run the risk of our free choice of evil instead of good.

Second, much of the physical evil in the world today, such as destruction of the environment, hunger, disease, etc., actually comes from our own fault, our own ignorant, greedy misuse of the world, and it seems God wants us to learn from our own mistakes how to be more responsible stewards of the material world—and our own bodies—he has entrusted to us.

But there is no doubt that there is still a great deal of inevitable suffering, disasters, accidents, death built into the structure of a dynamic evolving material world, in which vulnerable body-bound living beings, either lacking intelligence entirely or of very limited intelligence, are challenged to feel their own way toward higher growth by the unpredictable interplay of fixed natural laws and chance interactions—*if* God wishes to try the magnificent experiment of creating such a world that ends with Christ and redeemed, risen, and glorified humanity. God has already created a much more perfect spiritual world, that of the angels or pure spirits, where there is no trace of any of the physical evils of our lowly world. But we have no right to forbid God to stretch his power and wisdom to the limit and make the daring decision to create a world beginning with the lowliest dimension of matter and then evolving upward to be finally inhabited by spirit, be transformed by it, and raised up to eternal blissful union with God himself. God never promises us that we will not be vulnerable or have to suffer along the way, only that he will be *with us* at every point along the way and take care, in his own way, of those who get hurt, either in this or the next life. We do not really have the right or the wisdom to declare it impossible for God to create any but worlds we consider perfect.

There is also the further mystery, which human experience bears out, I think, to all of us who have lived long enough, that somehow the full depth and richness of human character is simply not reached by embodied spirits like us unless by passing through the challenge, purification, and transformation of suffering. Herein lies part of the mystery of the Cross and the passion of Jesus himself.

A brief further word here about the question of how God could allow a world where life and death are woven so closely together, and where most living species live by devouring another in a constant cycle of life through death. I know this bothers the Course a great deal. There is plenty of mystery here, to be sure. But I think there is another way of looking at it than just an insane tale of horror and destruction. Living things below the human level are not persons possessing self-consciousness and freedom; hence, each individual is not an end in itself like persons, but is subordinated to a larger common good, ultimately for the good of persons. And one could well say that, rather than higher species just "killing" lower ones and so destroying the purpose of the lower ones, the lower ones are in fact fulfilling their purpose by "feeding" the higher ones, and that the constant struggle for survival is in fact the primary trigger behind the whole immense creative evolution of new forms of life in nature. But this question really deserves more time for careful discussion than we can give it here.

Even when all the above is said, we must be very honest and admit we cannot give adequate answers in this life to all the searching questions and objections brought forward by the Course about the problem of evil in our present world. Our Christian faith commits us to believing and trusting that God can somehow work through the allowance of evil to bring a greater good out of the whole process in the end, though we ourselves cannot see clearly yet what this will look like in detail.

In conclusion, we can only say that we certainly have here two profoundly different ways of looking at and judging the world we live in, in the light of the first article of the Christian Creed, the creation of all that is by God alone, and its basic goodness.

WAPNICK: Again, Norris, we could not agree more on how these two spiritualities do *not* agree. If I may, I should like to expand on some of the points I made earlier, specifically applying them to this important problem of evil.

22

We can speak of *A Course in Miracles* as a non-dualistic spirituality, while the Bible presents a dualistic one. I believe this distinction will be helpful in developing our thesis of how radically different these two spiritualities are from each other.

In terms of creation, there cannot be both good *and* evil in the Course's view of reality, because there is only God. The phenomenon of opposites exists only in the illusory world of perception and matter, which God did not create. And as *A Course in Miracles* says in the Introduction to the text: "The opposite of love is fear, but what is all-encompassing can have no opposite." And so the Course's non-dualistic God of creation is only Love, which means that evil does not exist since there can be nothing *but* the Love of God.

However, evil, which in *A Course in Miracles* is equated with the belief in sin and separation from our Source—God—most definitely does exist in the dualistic, post-separation world of dreams. But since all this occurs only within the collective and individual dreams of the world, sin and evil cannot and do not truly exist, because only a mis-thought in a dreaming mind believes it can will in opposition to the Will of God, and bring into existence a world of multiplicity. Therefore within his fevered dream of sin, the Son actually believes that he has destroyed the oneness of Reality, which he judges to be an evil act deserving only punishment.

I should also like to emphasize that the mind that is referred to in *A Course in Miracles* is not the human mind. The mind antedates the making of the world, and thus comes before all forms—both animate and inanimate. That is why the Course teaches that all things in the world are equally unreal, and that "there is no life outside of Heaven" (text, p. 459; T-23.II.19:1). While it would take another book to discuss this in depth, it is important at least to note this because it highlights another important difference. The God of the Bible is most definitely a person, while the God of *A Course in Miracles*—though spoken of *as if* "He" were a

23

person, is in reality totally beyond all such anthropomorphisms. Thus, the biblical God takes on very human characteristics and motives—both high and low—and all this is
taken to be literally true by the Christian. In the Course, on
the other hand, the student is asked to understand that these
anthropomorphisms are metaphorical or symbolic, and not to
be understood as literally true.

I cannot emphasize enough that the God of *A Course in
Miracles* is not a person or a human being, and therefore does
not reason or think like one. From the Course's perspective,
all such biblical references are anthropomorphic projections
of the ego thought system onto the figure of God. Moreover,
to make the point again, evil has no place in a non-dualistic
reality, and so God cannot know about it nor, obviously, react
to it. His very non-dualistic being is evil's undoing.

I think we have made the differences clear in regard to creation, so let us move on to a discussion on the nature of Jesus.

CLARKE: Before we move on, could we go back to the
Course's teaching on the origin of the world through the falling asleep of divine consciousness? This is something that
has clear echoes for me of the ancient Gnostic theories. The
early Fathers of the Church strongly criticized the Gnostics
because of that, what they called the "tale of the origins,"
which the Fathers considered a myth that could not stand up
to critical reflection.

It is this notion of a divine consciousness somehow falling
asleep that the Christian would have great difficulty with,
because on the one hand, the Course would say that the
material world is an illusion, so therefore God would have to
be pure spirit; but if you are pure infinite spirit it is very difficult to see what meaning "falling asleep" could have, because
that is a function of having a body, and blacking out, and
going down into the unconscious. You cannot have that without a body. So, on the one hand, it seems God would have to
be conceived of as material—as having a body—in order to

fall asleep. On the other hand, that would have to be denied. So the notion of a divine, pure, infinitely perfect and happy consciousness somehow falling asleep or being divided against itself is an extremely difficult one to make sense out of for a philosopher, let alone a Christian believer.

WAPNICK: I think part of the answer to that, which does not resolve the difference certainly, is that, according to the Course, "falling asleep" is not something that happens to a body. The Course's understanding is that it would be a purely mental activity, and the falling asleep would really be tantamount to the belief that we could be separate from God. The thought of separation is defined by *A Course in Miracles* as the beginning of the dream. The body comes later, once the physical world is "miscreated," as the Course would say. But the act of falling asleep, in the view of *A Course in Miracles*, would be the equivalent of the mind's having that thought of being separate from God. The Course's position is that that is an impossible thought: how could part of God separate from Himself? Or as you would say, how could part of Christ fall asleep, if His nature is in being awake? And the Course's answer to that, which does not logically answer the question, is that it is an impossible thought and therefore it never really happened: we just believe that the impossible has occurred. In fact, there isn't even a "we" who *could* believe it. I realize the tremendous philosophical problems that presents, and I think it is a premise that defies logic. Indeed, these same problems can be traced from Plato on through the history of Christian philosophy.

In fact, *A Course in Miracles* says that even raising this as a question is an ego ploy, really being a statement masquerading as a question; the statement being: I believe I exist as a separated self, and now I want you to explain to me how I got here. Thus it is only an ego that would ask such a question, and even answering this pseudo-question is tantamount to supporting the basic ego premise that the separation indeed did occur. Therefore, once the question is granted validity, it would become our job to try to understand it, which is patently impossible. At one point in the Course, Jesus states that we still believe our "understanding is a powerful contribution to the truth, and makes it what it is" (text, p. 356; T-18.IV.7:5). In other words, we should not attempt to understand something that is inherently un-understandable.

Therefore, what *A Course in Miracles* is trying to do is *describe*, not *explain*, how we ended up here, and if I may go back to something you were saying a moment ago, Norris: The fact that God is spirit, formless, and perfect, the Course uses as its explanation for why God could not have created this world. In other words, this world *is* imperfect and is a world of form and bodies, change and death: evidence the Course uses as proof that God could not and indeed could never have created it, since He could create only like Himself. *A Course in Miracles* begins with the premise that anything God creates must share in His attributes and characteristics, and since this physical world and the body do not share in the attributes and characteristics of God, He therefore could not have created it.

CLARKE: Kenneth, that is a very interesting and revealing statement, that helps us to get behind some of the profound differences in world-vision between the Course and traditional Christianity. According to the Course, God could only create something perfect like himself, and that would exclude a world not only of evil but also of imperfection, change, bodies (matter) and death.

Although Christian revelation itself does not go into these more philosophical questions explicitly, it has an implicit attitude which Christian theologians have always clearly taught. First, since God is an infinitely perfect being, it is absolutely impossible for him to create another infinitely perfect being like himself. An infinite being can only be one, unique. A second such would have to be lacking something of what the first had, hence not be infinite, or else coincide perfectly with the first infinite being and so be identical with it. So any world that God creates in any way distinct from him will have to be imperfect in some way. And if it is a world of pure spirits, if these are to be real persons, they must have intelligence and free will (that is what a spiritual being means) and so are open to freely rejecting or resisting God in some way, thus opening the way for at least some moral evil in the world.

But the real sticking point, I think, is the possibility of God creating a material world and its being good and in some way an image of himself. To expand on a point we talked about earlier: A Christian (and many other religious people, Jews, Moslems, etc.) would say we cannot limit God's creativity, and that God takes delight in stretching his power all the way to the limit and creating lowly beings all the way down the spectrum of being into matter, and then lifting up this world of matter slowly by the progressive penetration of spirit into it, finally up into the partial light of spiritual consciousness in human beings, and then transformed by the resurrection into the light of glory with God, with the risen Jesus as the forerunner. God delights in taking the lowliest things and raising them up to the heights. He delights, one could say, in working as an artist in matter, and all true art is the penetration and illumination of matter by spirit. Matter can indeed be the carrier and the symbolic expression of spirit. If every authentic human artist can do this, so even more can God, the ultimate model and inspiration of all artists. And we can't, with our limited human imaginations, tell God he cannot do that. God has already undoubtedly created many other more perfect, perhaps purely spiritual universes, including our own angelic one. But he wants also to show his creative power by this daring experiment with an evolving material world, with spirit slowly emerging from within it, full of imperfection, false starts, slips, etc., but on the move toward being taken up finally into the higher life of spirit.

God can indeed imprint his image, however dimly, on this material world and love this humble work of his hands as filled with actual and potential goodness.

This is where, it seems to me, the deep Gnostic inheritance of the Course comes out, for this whole tradition has always had a deep distrust and denigration of matter, as something evil or at least unworthy of God's attention and love. For the Christian, on the other hand, God loves this lowly expression of himself and loves to work creatively with it, though always with the view of penetrating it with spirit, such as is shown by all the intelligible forms, structures, order, harmony and splendor of beauty shining forth from our lowly material world.

WAPNICK: Before responding to your overall comment, Norris, I would like to clarify one point you just made by reiterating my earlier comment. To be sure, *A Course in Miracles* would teach that the body is "unworthy" of God—in fact, it refers to the body as a "travesty" and "parody" of God's creation—but it certainly does not see the body as evil, as did many of the Gnostics. This would give the body a reality it does not have, for if you are nauseated or repulsed by something—as so many of the Gnostics certainly were by the body—you obviously must believe in its reality. And thus these Gnostics gave a psychological reality to what they philosophically did not believe in. *A Course in Miracles* does not fall into that very subtle and clever ego trap.

And now to your main point, Norris, which you have so eloquently expressed, and which is the crux of the issue: the anthropomorphic view of God that is inherent in all of Christian theology. I have already addressed this, but let me add some comments. While the Course does not directly discuss this, what I say would logically follow from the Course's principles.

We would both agree that God is an infinitely perfect being. However, we certainly would disagree on what this really means. For *A Course in Miracles* this means that God is not an individual, with a personal identity or self; that is, He has no form that sets Him off from His creation. He is thoroughly impersonal, as is Plotinus' One. Thus, His uniqueness is not defined by comparing Him with another, but rather God is unique because there *is* no other. And as the Course teaches, there is nowhere where the Father ends and the Son begins as something separate from Him (workbook, pp. 237-38; W-pI.132.12:4), since they are one.

Moreover, the Course's God does not think in the manner we would call thought, nor does He plan or take delight in anything. He is Totality—the All—and no "thing" can exist outside Him. Therefore, He certainly does not experience Himself in relationship to His creation. Creation, in *A Course in Miracles*, can be defined simply as the extension of God's being as spirit, which is as formless, changeless, and eternal as Himself. Since we are talking about a non-dualistic dimension that is beyond space and time, it would be impossible for us to conceive of what this creation is really like. Again, I am reflecting the Course's non-duality, which would not allow the kinds of statements you have made about God.

Finally, I just want to underscore this crucial difference in *A Course in Miracles* relative to Christianity: in no way, in the Course's view of reality, could matter ever be the carrier of spirit, nor be its expression. Spirit and matter are mutually exclusive states, only one of which is real. We are thus back again to our statement of the non-duality of *A Course in Miracles'* teachings.

CLARKE: I might mention again that there also seem to me profound echoes of non-dualistic Vedanta in Hinduism. For it, too, the descent into multiplicity in separation from the one God, Brahman, who alone truly is and is "One without a second," is really a fall into *maya*, the world of illusion, which really can never be explained.

WAPNICK: Yes, there are a lot of similarities between *A Course in Miracles* and the Vedanta teachings, as well as the highest teaching of Buddhism. In fact, some people have referred to the Course as the Christian Vedanta.

CLARKE: Who referred to it that way?

WAPNICK: Bill Thetford was someone who did. He was the psychologist who had worked with Helen Schucman, the scribe of the Course.

CLARKE: I see. So, were they both aware of that?

WAPNICK: Not at the time, but as soon as *A Course in Miracles* started coming through to Helen from Jesus, and Bill began reading it, he began to do a lot of reading on his own on the mystical teachings of both the East and the West. And it was at that point that he discovered that the Course had some commonalities with the Vedanta.

CLARKE: So they hadn't studied that previously?

WAPNICK: No. Neither of them had any background in Eastern thought at all.

CLARKE: That's amazing.

WAPNICK: And neither of them had any background in Gnosticism. It was not until I began doing the research for my book (*Love Does Not Condemn*) that I realized the extent of Gnostic language and metaphysical ideas in the Course. It was rather startling to me, actually, to see some of the parallels.

What I have also found, which is an important part of my book and which I think you would be particularly interested in, is that—to my way of thinking—the Course resolves a basic paradox that has run through most of Platonic thought: namely, how you get from the perfect One and Good to the world of imperfection and multiplicity. I know that that was a paradox that the philosopher Plotinus never resolved—a kind of tension running through his work. Where the Platonists and Neoplatonists ended up was somehow concluding that despite all of the antipathy they felt towards the body and many aspects of the world, the cosmos and the body did ultimately proceed from the One, from God. And from the point of view of *A Course in Miracles,* that presents a paradox again: how this perfect God, Who is pure spirit, formless, and eternal, can somehow end up creating a world that does not share in those characteristics.

To restate this point briefly, the Course's resolution is that the imperfect universe of duality is simply a dream that we—as a collective, not individual mind—are dreaming. Once we awaken from the dream we realize that it was only a dream of separation that never truly happened. The integrity of the non-dualistic Godhead thus remains intact. I realize that we are going around in the same circle, and that from what you are saying, Norris, this point of view—which to the Course is crucial—is not a problem to the Christian.

CLARKE: I have already expressed the Christian position on God's creation of a material world. But the astonishing affinity between the Course and these very ancient doctrines like Gnosticism and Hindu Vedanta shows there is a natural inclination in human culture towards this mode of thinking.

I might also add that even in mainstream Western thought, in the very influential school of Neoplatonism (founded by Plotinus in the third century A.D., the last great pagan school of philosophy before the triumph of Christianity with the conversion of the Roman Emperor Constantine), there was a significant strain of Gnosticism, despite Plotinus' explicit criticism of it, in that human souls were considered to have fallen down into the prison of matter as a result of pulling away from their previous blissful union with God as pure spirits in heaven, seeking their own independence. But Plotinus had a somewhat similar problem as in the Course, about why souls already apparently united to God in bliss should wish to break away. He could never quite come up with a satisfactory explanation, alternating between a punishment for sin and a positive mission to the alien world of matter to beautify it by the government of soul.

For the Christian, however, there is no falling away of pure spiritual souls from any pre-bodily state of union with God. This position was condemned early in Christian history as contrary to Christian revelation. Human souls are created for the first time in bodies as their natural complement, in an imperfect but good state, to make their way by a journey through the material world, as a place of education and testing, to their final home with God in transformed bodies. The original goodness of human nature has been weakened, shadowed over, made more vulnerable (destroyed or corrupted according to Lutheran Christianity) by the human race's free turn into sin, with its inherited consequences.

WAPNICK: Again, I think the differences are clear. *A Course in Miracles'* point of view, to state it once more, is that all this is occurring within the dream. There is a line in the Course that says "You are at home in God, dreaming of exile" (text, p. 169; T-10.I.2:1). There is another line, originally stated by Mary Baker Eddy, the founder of Christian Science, which quotes her comment that in the Book of Genesis in the Bible we are told that a deep sleep fell upon Adam, but nowhere else in the story does it say that he awoke (text, p. 15; T-2.I.3:6). I think this is another way of making the same point. We could say, metaphorically, that everything that happened since "Adam fell asleep" would be relegated to the dream. Thus, everything that we experience within the billions and billions of years of the dream we call evolution are the effects of the thought that we could pull off the impossible; i.e., that we could be First Cause by killing off our Source, usurping God's role as First Cause, and then "proving" it by making up a world of opposites and multiplicity.

The core of this ego dream is the body, what *A Course in Miracles* refers to as "hero of the dream." And there is nothing positive about it, the body being made to protect the ego's thought of separation and therefore attack the oneness of God's Love. On the other hand, once the dream has begun, the body becomes neutral, serving either the ego's purpose of imprisoning the mind in the thought system of separation— sin, guilt, and fear; or the Holy Spirit's aforementioned purpose of having it serve as a classroom in which we learn the lessons of forgiveness and awaken from the dream.

Thus on Level One the body is understood as an illusion of separation, hate, and a limitation on limitless Love, of which God knows nothing; on Level Two, it is seen as an illusion that serves either a harmful or helpful purpose, and with the latter, our experience is that Jesus or the Holy Spirit is an ever-present help.

CLARKE: That makes much clearer to me the teaching of Level One of the Course. But I must add that even if there could be such a state of turning away from God to think up an illusory or "dream" world, it would seem to me that God himself, with his infinitely perfect knowledge to which "everything lies uncovered and open," even the innermost thoughts of man (Heb 4:13), would have to know clearly (far more than a human father could about his child's nightmare) that the soul is dreaming and what kind of illusion it is dreaming up, since this is a positive act of a real mind, and then God would seek in compassionate love for us to come and help us awaken. The Christian God knows all of our ignorance, dreams, illusions, etc., and has precisely sent his Son Jesus to lead us from darkness to light.

JESUS

Nature and Role

CLARKE: The second major difference between the Course and traditional Christianity that we have to bring into the clear concerns who Jesus really is and his mission on earth. According to Christianity, Jesus is literally the Son of God who has taken on a real, bodily human nature like ours through Mary of Nazareth, his human mother, to walk the human journey with us, give up his life for us freely, though innocently, by taking the burden of our sins upon himself and dying on the cross, and then rising again with a real glorified body to live forever in immortal glory with God his Father and thus offer us, too, a share forever in his own happiness. This is the second great article of faith in the Christian Creed.

For those not familiar with Christian teaching, a further word may be needed as to what is meant when it is said that Jesus is "the Son of God," and returns to "God his Father" in heaven after his life on earth. Christianity believes with Judaism, from which it sprang, that there is but one God, one divine being of infinite fullness of perfection, creator of all that is not God. But it also holds, as revealed by Jesus himself, that the inner life of this one God is an intensely active one, that God actively thinks up a perfect thought image or inner expression of himself so complete and perfect that it, too, becomes a person and receives this ecstatic self-expression with gratitude and love, and for this reason is called the "Word" or "Son" of the "Father" from whom it proceeds, totally identical in all perfection with the self-thinking source from which it proceeds, except that it is *from* the Father and so distinct from him as his inner self-*expression*.

These two inner personal poles of the divine life then unite in a single ecstatic act of love of the divine goodness and each other as possessing it, an act of love which is a self-expression through love—a love image—of the same divine being, again so total and complete that it, too, becomes a person and becomes a third inner pole within the divine life like the second person, and so is called by the mysterious name of "Holy Spirit" (the one breathed forth by love). All this takes place still remaining within the unity of the one divine being, but it reveals God to us not as a solitary person but as an infinitely rich and active inner circulation of life among three mutually knowing and loving persons, the ultimate fullness of what it really means to be. Now when God takes on our human nature in Jesus the man, who is supposed to express the divine in human form, it is fitting that it be the Second Person, the perfect divine image or self-expression, who takes on this human nature as his own, to be the image of God on earth, and transform us also by union with him to become images or "adopted children of God." That is why it is said that "the Son of God became man." This doctrine of God as "Triune" or "Trinity" (one God in three persons) is the background for understanding the doctrine of Jesus as Son of God become man.

This understood, let us simplify and get right down to the basic disagreement. For Christian faith, Jesus is a *divine person* who has taken on a human nature (without losing his divine nature of course) to lead us back to God as our teacher and redeemer from sin, the one who through baptism makes us "adopted children of God." And he has taken on a *real body*, which he will hold on to in a transformed or glorified form through all eternity since his resurrection from the dead. We, too, will finally be with him and like him also with real, though glorified, bodies.

For *A Course in Miracles*, on the contrary, Jesus is not himself divine, has no divine nature. Rather, he is part of the original Christ consciousness that broke off from God, but is the first one to have awakened from this illusory dream state of so-called separation from God and has become a loving teacher to help the rest of us wake up from this dream, too. So he does not truly have a real body as a permanent part of his being, but only appears to have, to us who are still caught in the dream. The figure of Jesus is a wonderful and beloved figure in the Course, but is still radically different in nature from the Jesus of traditional Christianity, and it is important to recognize this clearly and not fudge it over as though it were merely a different way of saying the same thing. I think that you, Kenneth, with your admirable honesty and desire for clarity, would be the first to admit this.

WAPNICK: Yes, that's correct, Norris. I think that is probably one of the clearest and most distinct differences, in addition to the origin of the world, that one would find between *A Course in Miracles* and traditional Christianity. "Christ" in the Course does not refer only to Jesus, but to the collective Sonship of which Jesus and each of us—as mind—is a part. The Course basically teaches that when the Son seemed to fall asleep—it would never say, once again, that the Christ consciousness, or a part of it, broke off or fell asleep—the dream of seeming separation began. The difference between Jesus and the rest of the Sonship is that he was the first, as he states in the Course, to have awakened from the dream and to remember who he is as Christ. *A Course in Miracles* never really gets into *when* he does this; that is irrelevant to our discussion. But on the level of spirit, he is no different from us. In this world, he is the elder brother who in effect reaches back and helps everyone to do what he has already accomplished. There is no question that there is a clear theological difference in the two traditions, and this can be best understood by a discussion of the Course's concepts of specialness and the body.

From the beginning of Christian theology, Jesus was conceived as ontologically different from the rest of creation. As your comments reflect, Norris, Jesus is believed by the Churches to be the *only* Son of God, while according to Pauline theology, all other humans are considered to be adopted sons. This would violate the Course's principle of the non-duality of Heaven and the oneness of God's creation— Christ—by establishing God as the Creator of a hierarchy of beings. In this chain of being, Jesus is first and everyone else is beneath him, as lesser children. And then of course there is the rest of physical creation, set beneath homo sapiens as described in the first two chapters of Genesis.

"Specialness" is the Course term for the fundamental ego belief that others—beginning with God—are more special than we, and that we *need* their special attributes to compensate for our own inherent lack. Central to the treatment of specialness in *A Course in Miracles* is the emphasis placed upon the body. It is the body, in the Course, that is the embodiment of the ego's thought system, for it always highlights the separating differences or specialness among people, rather than the sameness we all share. And so, again from the Course's perspective, the Church's emphasis on Jesus' body would fall right in line with the ego's plan to make its thought system real. That is why Jesus states in the Course that he would not offer us his body, but his mind, since that alone is what is important (T-19.IV-A.17:5-6; not in first edition). Moreover, since spirit and flesh, Heaven and the world, are mutually exclusive states—one real, the other illusory—the biblical notion of incarnation, absolutely central to Christian faith, would be inconceivable and impossible. In fact, in one place *A Course in Miracles* states that, strictly speaking, the Word of God cannot be made flesh, since it involves "the translation of one order of reality into another" (text, p. 141; T-8.VII.7:2).

But where *A Course in Miracles* and traditional Christianity have a lot in common, however, is in feeling Jesus to be an inner and loving presence of God, to whom we turn as a beloved friend and brother. Indeed, the Course makes it very clear that without Jesus (or the Holy Spirit), changing one's mind through forgiveness—*A Course in Miracles'* definition of salvation—would be impossible. On that level, I think we would see many commonalities, and some passages in the Course echo what many Christians feel towards Jesus.

Nonetheless, here too we would see a difference between our two spiritual systems. Since the world and body are illusory, and therefore all of our experiences here are part of the ego's dream, it would make no sense for Jesus to be helping us live within a dimension that is inherently unreal. Rather, in the teachings of *A Course in Miracles*, Jesus is understood as being only within our *minds,* as a thought of love. Therefore, he is not really relating to us—person to person, or body to body—though we certainly experience him that way, relating to our individuality. His function is, quite simply, to *remind* us that we—the decision maker in our minds—are the dreamers of the dream, rather than the dream figures that we think of as our physical and psychological selves to which we give a name and assign a personal history.

It is always helpful to remember that according to *A Course in Miracles*, it is only within the mind that help is needed, for only then can we change our minds about who we truly are. And so, once again, Jesus is understood as not operating in the world—as he is definitely seen to be doing in Christianity—but only within the mind, where the dream has its origin and its existence. Therefore, the mind is the only place where mistakes can be undone. In the Course's language, Jesus does not work with the *effects*—the body, or behavior—but only with their *cause*—the decision made by our minds to identify with the ego's thought system.

CLARKE: Against this background of profound differences, I agree that there are some commonalities regarding Jesus. For example, there are some beautiful prayers of Jesus to God in the Course with which Christians could easily resonate and feel affinity. On the practical level, too, there are many spiritual and moral insights about attitudes toward others that Christians could find quite congenial, such as love, forgiveness, compassion rather than attacking others, the nature of "holy" rather than clinging relationships with people. The latter in particular I found both beautifully expressed and enlightening to me personally.

WAPNICK: That is why I talk about a Level One and Level Two.

The Meaning of the Crucifixion and the Resurrection

CLARKE: Thus far we have discussed the basic differences between the teaching of the Course and that of traditional Christianity on the meaning of creation, the reality and goodness of matter and bodies, the divinity of Jesus, and his having a real body, which at the resurrection was transformed into a glorified body and is now eternally with him in heaven—all of which the Course denies in some way or other. Let us now turn to the reality and meaning of the death of Jesus on the cross, the atonement for our sins resulting from his thus freely accepting death, and the reality of his bodily resurrection from the dead.

Traditional Christianity maintains that human beings have really sinned and turned away from God, hence have the burden of a genuine (not merely neurotic) guilt, needing to be forgiven by God. Then Jesus took on the burden of our own sins and truly suffered and died on the cross to make reparation for them. He then truly rose from the dead, with a real, though transformed or glorified body, and is forever united with his Father now in glory, with his whole risen and transformed humanity, body and soul.

The Course, on the other hand, teaches that since we never really separated ourselves from God by sin, but only in thought in an illusory dream experience which gave birth to the ego, there is no real guilt to be forgiven by God. What is called the forgiveness of human sin by God is really only our waking up from the dream with the help of Jesus to realize we were never separated from God in the first place and have never lost his love, which remains perfectly unchanged toward us. Then, since Jesus did not have a real body, but only appeared to for those within the dream world, he did not really suffer and die on the cross, but only appeared to, and was never really affected by what seemed to be the suffering inflicted on him by sinful men. Furthermore, he did not really atone for our sins, since these were not real in the first place. Finally, he did not really die in a real body, hence did not really rise again retaining his body in any form, since this is only the illusion of those in the dream. As we awake from the dream we will realize that he and we are both still united to God in a perfect union of love, and have always been so, and the whole bodily experience of ourselves and Jesus is a dream.

There is obviously a profound and irreconcilable difference here between the two views, which cannot be glossed over or explained away.

WAPNICK: I should like first to comment on your comments about the Course, Norris. I think your explanation of what it says is fine, with only one exception. In your account of Jesus, you make *A Course in Miracles* sound much too Gnostic. As we have seen, the Course is Gnostic in its cosmogony, but not in its view of Jesus. Certainly Jesus' body is illusory, but so is everyone else's. The difference is that he knew it, while the rest of the world still remains asleep, believing that its dream is real. Jesus, as I have already said, was and is outside the dream, and yet remains aware of the dreams of his brothers and sisters. Therefore, he did not suffer, because he could not. To *A Course in Miracles*, pain and suffering are only realities within the dream. When one awakens from the dream, following Jesus' example, then all pain and suffering are impossible.

Returning now to your general comments about the crucifixion and resurrection, Norris, I think that we would agree on one level and not on another. Where *A Course in Miracles* and traditional Christianity would agree is on the importance of Jesus' life and teachings. Where we would disagree, however, would be on the nature and meaning of the crucifixion and resurrection, which I will get to right now. I do want to make it clear, however, that *A Course in Miracles* does not deny that within the world's dream Jesus was crucified. It does deny, however, the traditional interpretation of his crucifixion, and I think that when we get into discussing the resurrection, we will find very crucial differences between the Course and traditional Christianity.

Where I would like to begin is with the role of God in the redemptive plan, specifically in the crucifixion. What *A Course in Miracles* would say about what you explained—which certainly is the traditional way of looking at the crucifixion—is that such a view would have God see our sin, suffering, and evil as real. In other words, God perceives that we have indeed separated from Him by the act of disobedience that is portrayed in the Garden of Eden myth in the Book of Genesis. Therefore, He is essentially declaring our state of sinfulness to be ontologically real, and His sense of justice compels Him to cast us all out of paradise as punishment for Adam's sin of disobedience, which somehow also acknowledges that all of mankind has inherited this sin. Furthermore, as evil is now established as real in the world, God must devise a plan whereby His children can be saved. That plan, as you explained Norris, is to send His only begotten Son, Jesus, to die for our sins in an act of vicarious salvation and atonement through which the whole world is saved.

A Course in Miracles' position, again as you articulated at the beginning, is that God does not even know about sin, separation, and the dream. In other words, it is a dream that is outside His Mind and therefore does not, and cannot exist. And I certainly understand how this would wreak havoc on the basic Christian faith, not to mention on the traditional Christian Creed.

So the Course's jumping-off point is that God does not even know His children as sinful. *A Course in Miracles* does state, however, that although we are guiltless in eternity, we are guilty in time (text, p. 221; T-13.I.3:2). In other words, in the world of illusion—within the dream—we feel guilty, because we have made guilt real as a result of our belief in sin. But that is from the point of view of the dream, of the separated Son of God. It is not the point of view of God in *A Course in Miracles.*

Thus the Course's view of the crucifixion is that Jesus was demonstrating to us that what the world defines as sinful—which really is the misthought of believing that we have attacked and even murdered God, Christ, and truth—has had no effect. The Love of God, which Jesus certainly does represent both within Christianity as well as in *A Course in Miracles,* is totally unaffected and unchanged by the ego's dream. And so basically the Course's position is that what Jesus did, in effect, was to provide the opportunity for God's children to reenact—within their dream—the sin of separating from God and attacking Him, usurping His place on the throne of creation, and finally killing Him and crucifying His Son. All these are the thoughts that began the dream, which inevitably led to the belief that the unified Love of God was capable of being destroyed by the Sonship's fragmenting it and making up a world of duality in its place.

In other words, when the world was confronted with the Love of God and the guiltlessness of His Son—in the person of Jesus—it attacked and crucified him. The charge biblically ascribed against Jesus was "blasphemy," since he taught, and still teaches us in *A Course in Miracles* that God's Son is sin-less and guiltless. And so the ego thought system of sin and guilt cannot prevail against this truth. His resurrection, which I will define in a minute, then becomes the living witness to the fact that the Love of God cannot be destroyed, for other-wise how can anyone experience his post-crucifixion pres-ence? And despite the terrible things that we accuse ourselves of doing—of being sinful, evil creatures that have attacked and even destroyed God—Jesus shows us in *A Course in Miracles* that God's Love for us remains unchanged. In effect, the love that Jesus had for us before the dream of cru-cifixion is the same love that he had for us during this dream of crucifixion, and in fact, after his apparent death and resur-rection as well. In other words, nothing that the ego or the world has done has changed God's perfect Love. A dream has no effect on reality, and the reality of Jesus is outside the world's dream.

In this way, therefore, the Course defines this demonstra-tion of the invulnerability of God's Love—in its own particu-lar language—as the manifestation of the "principle of the Atonement": namely, that the separation from God never truly occurred; the Love of God has not been affected by what we believe we have done. Again, the Course does make the crucifixion an important part of the Atonement plan of the Holy Spirit, but it also sees it quite differently, as I have just explained. The crucifixion, as seen through the eyes of tradi-tional Christianity, has Jesus suffering and dying on the cross. *A Course in Miracles* would say that he could not have suf-fered because all suffering ultimately comes from the guilt in our minds. And since Jesus had no guilt, there was no suffer-ing: he perceived people's attack on him as only a call for the Love of God they believed they had denied and that they could never regain. The dream of crucifixion served only the purpose of demonstrating—in this one specific and seem-ingly horrific instance—that the seemingly horrific instant of separating from God did not truly happen. To state this central point once again: a dream can have no effect upon reality.

CLARKE: So his suffering would really be in their minds...not a real suffering.

WAPNICK: Yes, that's right, not a real suffering on Jesus' part, because, again, he is outside the dream, where there is no sin and no guilt. And therefore there can be no suffering. As you have pointed out, Norris, that would make *A Course in Miracles* very Gnostic in its interpretation of the crucifixion in some areas, especially the idea that Jesus did not suffer. He *appeared* to suffer because that was the projection of the people beholding the crucifixion. In other words, he was a figure in *their* dream, who *had* to suffer and die to expiate their own sins. So in their dreams they beheld him as being put on a cross. As he says in the Course:

> I became the symbol of your sin, and so I had to die instead of you. To the ego sin means death, and so atonement is achieved through murder. Salvation is looked upon as a way by which the Son of God was killed instead of you....No one can die for anyone, and death does not atone for sin (text, p. 383; T-19.IV-A.17:2-4,8).

Thus, the crucifixion of God's Son is the key to the world's dream. But Jesus knew that he could not suffer or be crucified because, still once again, he knew that he was not a part of the world's dream.

Another way of understanding this is to think of Jesus as a voice calling to his brothers and sisters from *outside* the dream, to awaken and come to where he is. Instead, the world continued its dream and brought him *into* it, thereby shaping him to its own contours. And so the real Jesus in our minds was lost, and replaced by a dream figure—in a body—that had to be crucified since that is the nature of the world's dream. In *A Course in Miracles*, Jesus presents us with another opportunity to choose again, to choose to leave the dream and return to him in our minds, so that we may all return home together to God.

The crucifixion was a teaching lesson to demonstrate to us that what we believed was an attack on God had no effect. And following the Course's logic, succinctly stated here, if the attack on God had no effect, then it could not really have happened. This reflects the principle of cause and effect, wherein if there is no effect, there can be, by definition, no cause; and since everything that exists must affect something else, if something is not a cause, it cannot exist.

Thus, what Jesus demonstrated for us is that sin has not really happened, not that sins have been forgiven in the traditional sense—i.e., that sin is real and then something happens and we are forgiven for it—but that sin never happened in reality. So that is *A Course in Miracles'* ultimate definition of forgiveness: that we are forgiven for what we believe we accomplished; i.e., separated from God, which is what in truth we have *not* done. It is our belief system, then, that gets changed, but in the eyes of God we never really left Him and so there is nothing to forgive.

CLARKE: The resurrection, then, would not be the transformation and taking up of the body into the permanent state with God.

WAPNICK: Correct. In other words, the position of the Course here, too, would be very Gnostic. In his second letter to the Corinthians, written around the middle of the first century, Paul is railing against those people who believed that the resurrection was not of the body (a kind of proto-Gnostic belief, certainly). *A Course in Miracles* would agree with these Corinthians, and teaches that the resurrection is the awakening from the dream of death. This means that the resurrection really is a change of mind: it has nothing whatsoever to do with the body. So that we would then say that the resurrection of Jesus occurred *before* the dream of physical crucifixion. Again, *when* it occurred is irrelevant; but I think for our purposes we could certainly say that, in distinction from the traditional teaching, the resurrection of Jesus occurred before the crucifixion and had nothing to do with the body.

CLARKE: And so what seemed to the disciples like genuine appearances of Jesus in a risen body were really only symbolic manifestations at that time of what he already was and had always been, a purely spiritual being.

WAPNICK: Yes. I think that what happened to the followers of Jesus who did have an experience of his presence, was that they experienced his love in their minds. One of the teachings of *A Course in Miracles* is that minds are joined—that bodies do not join, but minds are joined. So these followers experienced the love of Jesus and the presence of Jesus; but because they experienced themselves only as bodies, they could not conceive of Jesus not being a body, too. Thus they projected that inner experience of Jesus, and so their conscious experience was of Jesus as a risen *body*. But from the Course's point of view, that would really be just a symbol that would have spoken to those followers who felt the presence of Jesus in their minds, in the only form that they could have accepted and understood.

CLARKE: But in Jesus himself it would already be a state that he had possessed for a long time.

WAPNICK: Yes, but even more to the point, *A Course in Miracles* teaches that the body does not really exist. In other words, it does not live and it does not die; and therefore it would make no sense from the Course's point of view to talk about the resurrection of the body.

THE EUCHARIST

CLARKE: The next obvious point of difference that needs to be discussed is the Christian doctrine known as the sacrament of the Eucharist, or the Holy Eucharist, which includes the Eucharistic liturgical rite known as the Sacrifice of the Mass and the Real Presence of Jesus under the form of bread and wine venerated in the "tabernacles" of all Catholic—not all Christian—churches. This is a very particular doctrine of the Christian religion, unique to it, I believe. But there are basic differences among the various Christian Churches themselves on its meaning. All believe, in some form, in the consuming of blessed bread and wine, at least as a symbolical remembrance of what Jesus did at the Last Supper before he died, when he said, "Do this in memory of me" (Lk 22:19). But only the Roman Catholic, the Eastern Orthodox, the Anglicans, Lutherans, and perhaps some others believe that the bread and wine in the Eucharistic liturgy are really and truly transformed into the body and blood of Jesus, beneath the perduring appearances of bread and wine. It is only this strongest form of the doctrine, represented most explicitly by the Roman Catholic Church and the Eastern Orthodox Churches, that I feel competent to speak for here.

According to this doctrine, traditional from the earliest days of the Christian Church, the Eucharistic liturgy is the reenactment in symbolic form of the original redemptive sacrifice of Jesus, in imitation of Jesus' own initial enactment at the Last Supper, which he asked his followers to keep doing in memory of him. This is done when the ordained priest, speaking in the name of Christ the High Priest, eternally living now as risen and present at every Mass, pronounces the "words of consecration" in imitation of Jesus, which really and truly transform the inner reality of the bread and wine into the body and blood of Jesus, but veiled in mystery under the remaining appearances of bread and wine. So the same original victim and priest are present again, and the actual death of Jesus, which happened only once, is symbolically reenacted by the ritual separation of the body and blood in the separate consecrations of the bread and wine. The original real death of Jesus, here symbolically reenacted over and over again, is now really offered up anew each time at Mass. Then at the Communion service following, the believers partake of the body and blood of the sacrificed and now risen Christ under the appearances of bread and wine, in obedience again to Jesus' command, "Unless you eat my body and drink my blood you shall not have life in you ..." (Jn 6:53). Thus Jesus, just before he left his disciples in death, left a living memorial of himself to remain with them forever as their Bread of Life, his Real Presence under the outward appearances of bread and wine venerated in the tabernacles of all Catholic churches throughout the world and indicated by the "sanctuary lamp" always kept burning as long as the Blessed Sacrament is kept within.

This is indeed a complex and mysterious doctrine, a miracle completely beyond our minds to understand, and knowable only by faith. Only God himself could do such a miracle. I am not concerned to defend it here, but only to say what is believed, and to make the point that this has become the central focus of all Catholic worship down the ages, in obedience to the two original commands of Jesus to his disciples, "Do this in memory of me," and "Unless you eat my body and drink my blood...." There have been many attempted theological explanations of just what is going on here and how; but none of them can exhaust the depth and richness of the mystery, and none is mandatory on the believer.

It is clear that the Course, in terms of its own central doctrines, cannot accept any of this literally. And, in fact, I have noticed that often when Catholics join the Course, sometimes believing they can still remain Catholics, the first part of their

Catholic practice that drops off is their belief in the Eucharist and their attendance at Mass. For, since the Course teaches that the body of Jesus is not real, nor his death on the cross, there cannot literally be a transformation of bread and wine into his body and blood, nor any real reenactment of a death that never really took place. The sole authentic worship is the adoration and love of God himself, with whom we have always really been in blissful union. Once this is clearly understood, many misunderstandings and confusions can be avoided by followers of the Course. It is important to know what one is doing and do it wholeheartedly. Only thus can one please God.

WAPNICK: Certainly in discussing the Eucharist or any sacrament of the Catholic Church there would be clear differences in the positions of *A Course in Miracles* and the Church. In fact, there are several passages in the Course— some of them veiled, some of them not so veiled—that really are reinterpretations of the traditional meaning of the Eucharist and communion, and that would also strike at the basic difference we have been highlighting: the Course's teaching that the physical world and the body are illusory.

From the point of view of *A Course in Miracles*, seeking outside oneself for salvation is a principal characteristic of specialness, which I discussed earlier. The special love relationship is one in which we believe someone or some object outside ourselves has something we lack: the capacity to make us happy and peaceful, or the capacity to save us. And so we seek to take these special persons or objects in and make their holiness or power our own, thereby completing our inherent incompleteness with something outside us and therefore not truly our own. In this sense, a special relationship would hold whether one is considering a love object, food, alcohol, or the body of Jesus. Thus, listening to the voice of specialness, we would believe that we lack the holiness and innocence of Christ, our true Self, but Jesus has what is missing in us. Therefore, if we are to have it, we must get it from him by partaking in the sacrament of the Eucharist, a process that only reinforces this lack, but does not undo or heal it.

In *A Course in Miracles*, however, Jesus would teach us that the purpose of remembering him is to remember his mind that identified only with the Love of God. Therefore, he urges us to call upon his name and presence to help us choose against the ego so that our minds can be like his, filled only with the Love of God. And it is this process that *does* heal the belief in lack, not by covering it over, but rather by helping us to change our minds about who we truly are. Thus, Jesus is no different from us, but rather he urges us to choose like him, joining with his *mind*, and not his body. So from the Course's point of view, it would make no sense for Jesus to share his illusory body with us in communion.

Therefore, the Course's position regarding the Eucharist would be that once it was established by the desire for specialness, it became a symbol having the meaning of either the ego or the Holy Spirit, depending on the purpose that it serves: guilt or forgiveness. And so the ritual can be understood by students of the Course—*as they would understand anything else*—to be a symbol that could serve the Holy Spirit's purposes of forgiveness. He accomplishes this by correcting the past mistakes of separation and undoing our guilt—present only in the mind—over having made the body real as a defense against the Love of God. Outside of this purpose, however, there is no place in the Course's curriculum or spirituality for a specific ritual like the Eucharist.

CLARKE: Could you explain more specifically just what it would be a symbol of?

WAPNICK: Yes. In other words, a student of *A Course in Miracles* could see how the Holy Spirit can take the doctrine of the Eucharist and teach the exact opposite of what the

Church has taught. Rather than being a reenactment of the redemptive message of Jesus whose body suffered and died for our sins, the ritual of the Eucharist can be seen as symbolizing his sharing with us the love in his mind. His *mind* (*not* his body) was one of total forgiveness: total love for all of us, a love that contains as well our love for each other, since the mind of God's Son is inherently one. And it is with this mind of unified love that we wish to join.

Thus the form of the sacrament would now be expressing a totally different content, which is asking Jesus for help in shifting our perception to reflect his true message of forgiveness. In that sense, a Course student could view the Eucharist as a helpful symbol for some people, a reminder or memorial of the meaning of the crucifixion; namely, that while the body can be attacked and killed, such action has no effect on our relationship with God. In other words, our seeming sin of crucifying God's Son—ontologically as well as in Palestine—had no effect on the true presence of Christ's innocence in our minds.

Thus, *A Course in Miracles* itself does not really say whether Jesus actually said the biblical Eucharistic words at the Last Supper, or even whether there were a Last Supper or not. Nonetheless, it could certainly be concluded from everything the Course does state that *if* Jesus did say these words, they did not have the meaning that the Church has given them. That is why in the Course he comments:

> I do not want to share my body in communion because this is to share nothing. Would I try to share an illusion with the most holy children of a most holy Father? Yet I do want to share my mind with you.... Would I offer you my body...*knowing* its littleness? Or would I teach that bodies cannot keep us apart? (T-7.V.10:7-9; T-19.IV-A.17:5-6; not in first edition)

We can therefore see that *A Course in Miracles* has clearly shifted the focus of Jesus' message to his mind from his body, which was made to be something special by Christianity. Incidentally, as I said earlier, the focus on the body is always the hallmark of a special relationship, the Course's term for the ego's attempt to make a substitute for God and His Love.

To summarize then, we can see from the Course that it is Jesus' love—within his mind—that he shares with all of us, without exception or exclusion.

CLARKE: Then the Eucharist would not be the *Real Presence* of Jesus...

WAPNICK: Exactly. *A Course in Miracles* would be very clear about that, as it would be of any sacrament: God Himself does not act in this world through the different forms, whether it is bread, wine, or anything else. In the philosophical language of the Church, we would say that God is not *immanent* (or present) in the world; nor is He *transcendent* in the sense of being beyond the world He created, a world which would be perceived as truly there. In God, there is simply no world to be *in* or *beyond*. The words themselves make no sense within a non-dualistic reality.

In conclusion then, it should be noted that *A Course in Miracles* does not have a concept of the Eucharist at all, and this is but one more example of how radically different Jesus' teachings in the Course are from the Bible and traditional Christianity—Catholic as well as Protestant. However, again, a student could view the Christian symbol of the Eucharist, Catholic or Protestant, as a helpful symbol or metaphor to those who resonate to it. As you point out, Norris, the Catholic believes that the Eucharist is the *Real Presence* of Jesus, that his body and blood are actually present on the altar in the bread and wine, although that is not what most Protestants believe. However, what all Christians who venerate the rite of communion share is the idea that Jesus suffered and died for our sins, and through the shedding of his precious blood, our sins were remitted and we were saved. And that is what is recalled to mind during the service—Catholic or Protestant. And to state it once again, that doctrine is diametrically opposed to what Jesus teaches his students in *A Course in Miracles*.

And so for the student of *A Course in Miracles*, the Eucharist is totally irrelevant, for there is no vicarious salvation—atonement through suffering—to commemorate. Moreover, Jesus knew literally that nothing was happening to destroy him because nothing had happened to destroy the unity of God in the original moment of separation. The whole thing was just a dream with no effect on reality at all. And Jesus, again, is not part of that dream. His very being was not present in the dream to be crucified, the crucifixion being the core of the ego's dream, but not God's reality.

And so Jesus reminds all of us that our true being is not in the dream either. From the perspective of *A Course in Miracles* then, this is the message of the crucifixion: nothing happened, for love cannot be changed or destroyed. That is why this message is summarized in the Course with these words: "Teach only love, for that is what you are" (text, p. 87; T-6.I.13:2; italics omitted). And this love remains forever outside the world's dream of crucifixion.

Before moving on, Norris, there is one point which I think you alluded to and implied that should be emphasized. In your comments on the crucifixion earlier, I think you pointed out a difference between how you would see the crucifixion and the way that some of the medieval theologians might have seen it. In other words, one of the points on which the Course differs with Christianity is the idea that God punished Jesus because we were bad and that his death was a ransom, in effect, to pay God back for our sins against Him. I realize that in the post–Vatican II Catholic Church, as well as in some mainstream Protestant Churches, many thinkers have been moving away from that idea: they are not saying that Jesus did not suffer and die, but they are moving away from the notion that this was God's way of being paid back. I don't know how you would feel about that, but the Course makes a point about it. That's why I bring it up.

CLARKE: I'm glad you brought that up, Kenneth. I had meant to say something about it earlier when talking about the crucifixion of Jesus. Misinterpretation and misunderstanding are very easy here, and Catholic theologians themselves have not always helped. Some metaphors of Scripture, too, have lent themselves to easy misunderstanding. Such metaphors like "ransom," which occur here and there, are used to explain why Jesus died for our sins—as though a price had to be paid *to* someone, either to the devil or to God himself, to win our forgiveness; or as if some kind of bargain had to be made with God, who exacted the price of his Son's death and whose anger was appeased by seeing his Son suffer and die. St. Anselm in the twelfth century even worked out a whole theological theory of the redemption built on a kind of justice transaction between God and the human race, where Jesus fulfilled the debt that man could not pay, since an offense against the infinite dignity of God could only be repaid by someone of equally infinite dignity, like Jesus as divine-human.

I take such expressions as metaphors in the Scripture, which are never in fact spelled out literally as a debt or ransom paid *to* anyone. The theological explanations, like Anselm's which tried to build on a literal interpretation of such metaphors were well-intentioned indeed, and had a certain legal, logical appeal. But they gave the impression of a not very loving and compassionate God, rather of one insisting on justice, on "the pound of flesh," so to speak, and satisfied by seeing his own Son suffer. There was a point of truth in them, but it seemed to get buried in the justice perspective. Few, I believe, would hold such theories today. (No theological explanation, by the way, is mandatory on a Christian believer, who can simply remain in the mystery so tersely expressed by Jesus himself.) Let me spell out my own explanation, which roughly parallels most today.

God was not interested in exacting any ransom or debt to appease his wounded dignity. As St. Thomas Aquinas puts it, God is offended by our sins, not because his own dignity is in any way threatened or wounded—which is impossible for any creature to do—but only because our sins *hurt us*, and God does not want his beloved children to be hurt. God could well have forgiven us, if he wished, without any punishment or reparation for sin being made. God has chosen—and his Son has freely accepted out of love for us—the way of healing and forgiveness of sins through the vicarious suffering of his Son as a powerful way of teaching us two great lessons.

First is the appreciation by us of the intrinsic evil of sin, especially serious sin, which tends of its nature to the rejection or "putting to death" of God as far as it can. If no objective punishment at all is given for human sin, given our narrow self-centered viewpoint, we would well conclude that it really doesn't matter very much whether we sin or not; God doesn't really care one way or the other in his remote bliss. Humans somehow naturally feel that objective moral evil should in some way be punished to restore the order of wise justice in the world; this has been shown down through the history of human cultures, with the tradition of sacrifice for sin in so many religions, and of course strongly in the Jewish tradition out of which Christianity arose. Even children seem to have a natural feel for this, that something must be done in fairness to make up for something bad done. The free taking on of the guilt of our sins by the innocent Son of God is a highly dramatic way of showing all this and so moving us to stay away from such sin in the future.

Second, it is a powerful teaching of how deep is God's compassionate love for us, that God himself would freely take on himself the punishment we should have justly suffered, in order to bring us back from the darkness and addiction of sin to his love again. As John's Gospel tell us, "God so loved the world that he gave his only-begotten Son" that we might live (Jn 3:16), and "Greater love than this no man has than that he lay down his life for his friend" (Jn 15:13). Love shown through freely accepted suffering for one's beloved may be the only, or at least the most powerful, language that can get through to our human hearts as well as heads. Another important aspect of this plan is that the remedy for sin leaves us in a far better situation than we were before, namely, that by solidarity with Jesus through baptism we are joined with him not only in his death to sin but also in his rising to a new immortal life in glory with God as adopted children of God, as a sign that his love is greater than any sin can be. There is the further point, too, that when Christians have to go through their own sufferings, they can feel the comfort and strength that they do not have to go through these alone, but in solidarity with him, so that in fact there is a mysterious transformative power in suffering itself accepted in union with Jesus.

WAPNICK: This is another area where we can see clearly how diametrically opposed *A Course in Miracles* and the Bible truly are. For the Course, suffering is chosen by egos to reinforce the belief that they are bodies, separated from their Creator and everyone else, and cannot serve the purpose, as seen in Christianity, of bringing people closer to God, or reconciling them to Him. And therefore in the Course, Jesus is not understood as suffering for us, nor as joining with us in our suffering. However, he would have us understand that suffering is our choice, and not God's Will for us. It is not for the purposes of salvation.

Interestingly enough, while *A Course in Miracles* would use much of the same terminology you have used, it would give the words an entirely different meaning—same form, but different content. So that where the Course might agree that the purpose of the crucifixion was to restore justice, the big difference would come in understanding what that justice truly is, and how it is restored. And this is still another example of how the Course uses terminology that has had specific meanings within Christianity, but gives it a meaning that is exactly the opposite of what has been traditionally understood.

A Course in Miracles would say that true justice is our acceptance of the truth that we have never left God, and that that is God's judgment of us: We are still His beloved child and, in truth, the ego dream of sin, guilt, and fear has done nothing to change that fact. And what the crucifixion did, again, was to provide the opportunity to reenact this dream for us, and for Jesus to manifest this judgment of God—that nothing happened to come between His children and His love—as the answer to it.

Psychologically, *A Course in Miracles* would certainly agree with what you are saying, Norris, that God Himself would not be offended by what we did. But the Course, once again, would take it one step further and say that God does not even know about what we did, or better, believed we did. The redemptive process exists only from our point of view. To the Course, God is not the architect of that plan, because from His point of view, the dream would simply be what it is—a dream—so that there is no evil that has to be redeemed. In other words, what has to be redeemed is our *thinking* that we have sinned, and our *belief* that we are evil.

To summarize, therefore, justice in Christianity is God's response to the sin that is real, while in *A Course in Miracles*, justice means that sin never occurred and that God's Son remains as He created him: sinless, guiltless, and perfect.

And so, to make the point again, suffering is not the Will of God, as it is in Christianity. Nonetheless, in the Course Jesus makes it clear that what he calls "periods of unsettling" are very often the inevitable effect of the process of forgiveness, which asks us to look at the very ego thoughts we have sought to deny and escape from (manual, p. 10; M-4.I.7). And this process of having to confront our deepest fears is almost always experienced as uncomfortable.

LIVING IN THE WORLD

CLARKE: This topic gives us a chance to discuss the second level in the Course, the actual dream life we are all involved in now, which for those within it has to be coped with seriously, as though it were real. Earlier we talked about the origin of the dream, at the first level. Now we are down on the practical level, in the midst of the human fray, so to speak. One of the main differences between the Course and traditional Christianity that emerges here is the conception of free will and the moral order, based on free personal moral decision, in which we differ from the animals.

For traditional Christianity, this life must be a very real one, because it is the theater of morality, which requires genuine personal moral responsibility, based on free moral decision, hence the exercise of free will. Now in a dream, as ordinarily understood, there is no moral responsibility, because we cannot exercise free choice. We are like observers, with life flowing by as a spectacle, not responsible actors in the play, because we cannot reflect self-consciously on what we are doing and be responsibly in charge of our actions—in a word, moral agents. Hence it would seem, in the Course's view, that the whole realm of freedom and morality would disappear, together with real moral evil (sin) and guilt. Could you shed some further light on this?

WAPNICK: Let me begin my response to your question, Norris, by stating clearly that the Course places a very strong emphasis on our free choice here within the dream, and the unequivocal necessity of our accepting responsibility for this. As Jesus urges his students to say:

> I am responsible for what I see.
> I choose the feelings I experience, and I decide
> upon the goal I would achieve.

> *And everything that seems to happen to me*
> *I ask for, and receive as I have asked.*
> (text, p. 418; T-21.II.2:3-5)

And this choice simplifies to the decision between the ego or the Holy Spirit as our guide for behavior. It is therefore *not* that our behavior in the world is unimportant to the Course. But rather that our *behavior* is understood as the result of our choosing the teacher in our *minds* that we wish to guide us throughout each day of our lives. It is this choice of the mind that is the focus of *A Course in Miracles*. This must be clearly comprehended by both students of the Course as well as its critics, otherwise its teachings will be seriously misunderstood. This is the misunderstanding that comes from the mistake of confusing the metaphysical and practical levels we have spoken of—Levels One and Two—and which we'll return to again later.

Therefore, I think that again, we could agree and disagree. Indeed, it could be said that on the metaphysical level, *A Course in Miracles* does not truly present us with a system of morality, at least not as the term is generally used. On this level, therefore, the Course offers no specific code of behavior because behavior is seen as merely the epiphenomenon of the thoughts in the mind, and it is the thoughts that need to be changed—in other words, guilt replaced by love through the process of forgiveness. Therefore, to focus only on a moral code would be committing, in the Course's terminology, the mistake of making the error real, since you would not be attempting to legislate or control behavior unless you *first* believed that problems came from the body and not the mind, and therefore these problems had to be solved on that physical level.

A Course in Miracles is emphatic in its teaching that it is the mind or thoughts that are the true problem—the cause—while the experienced problem remains the effect. This is certainly not to say that in our society we do not need laws and standards by which to live. For example, if parents are to fulfill their responsibilities as mother and father, there have to be firm guidelines in the home. Similarly, in a classroom, if rules are not reinforced by teachers and school administrators, the inevitable chaos would make learning impossible. And just as clearly, if there were no traffic laws, safe driving would be unthinkable. All this goes without saying, and nowhere in *A Course in Miracles* does Jesus ask us to deny this aspect of our daily living, even if the world, metaphysically speaking, is ultimately a dream.

Moreover, the Course's metaphysics is certainly not meant to lead to the conclusion that unloving actions are to be condoned or excused, and left to go unchecked. But it is to say, and in fact Jesus does make this very specific point in the Course, that simply changing or controlling one's behavior— as is the aim of any code of morality—is not enough, since the root cause that is the mind's guilt will still be there. It is this guilt that must be changed and replaced by the Love of the Holy Spirit that is already present. Once guilt has been entirely undone, only love remains in our minds, and therefore everything we do would be loving.

Thus, Jesus asks us to look at our ego choices to use our various worldly roles to reinforce separation and guilt, but to look at these choices with his love beside us. This enables us to accept his forgiveness for our mistakes, and thus to accept his love as our true identity. This means that we must accept responsibility for our decision to choose the ego as our teacher, which is the cause of our unloving behavior. And by accepting this responsibility for the power of our minds to choose wrongly, we are able to access this power of our minds to choose again and make the right choice at last.

This is such an important issue, and one that is so easily misunderstood, let me say it again. *A Course in Miracles'* metaphysical teachings of the fundamental unreality of the physical world should never be taken to mean that certain external restrictions on people's "ability to miscreate," to borrow a phrase from the Course, cannot be very helpful. It is simply the fact that these limits, *in and of themselves,* will not be able to effect a change at the mind level that is the only cause of true healing, and the only hope for a life that reflects the true love and peace of Jesus.

All too often, to repeat this point, people mistakenly believe that by controlling their behavior they can actually change their thoughts. And then what happens is that the underlying guilt and hatred which have not changed at all become projected out in the form of judgment or persecution, with the person being totally unaware of the true nature of his or her actions because the underlying thought has remained unconscious. This, for example, would be the Course's explanation for the otherwise inexplicable behavior of well-meaning Christians throughout history carrying out such vicious and anti-Christian actions as the Crusades or Inquisition in the name of the Prince of Peace. Their *unconscious* thoughts of attack and separation left these followers of Jesus in a state where they literally knew not what they did, and ended up justifying attack and murder by believing it was the Will of God.

It is not the dream itself that is the problem, but the unhealed thoughts in the mind of the dreamer. And it is these thoughts that are the source of what the world calls immorality, and their correction would be what *A Course in Miracles* would think of as true morality.

Now I can talk about the Course's concept of free will.

CLARKE: You have to bring the ego in, too; we haven't brought that in yet in a systematic way.

WAPNICK: Yes, we'll do that here. On one level, which is the level of Heaven, there is no free will as it is usually spoken or written about. When we speak of free will, we are clearly implying that there is a choice: I am free to choose love or fear, forgiveness or hatred, etc. In Heaven, a state of undifferentiated unity where opposites do not exist, there can be no choice from the Course's point of view. So that free will, the traditional understanding of it, would make no sense in Heaven.

CLARKE: St. Thomas says that in heaven, in the beatific vision, there would be freedom—in the sense that our whole selves would spontaneously go to God, but there would not be free choice; yet there certainly is along our earthly journey toward this goal, which is the realm of morality.

WAPNICK: Yes, and *A Course in Miracles* would actually agree. There is a section near the end of the text that is entitled "Freedom of Will," which says that our will, as it is one with God's, is free, but not in the sense of being free to choose because there is no choice, as we are both saying. Thus it is really a statement, again, of the undifferentiated and non-dualistic unity of Heaven. The will of God's Son is free because it cannot be otherwise. It cannot truly be imprisoned by the belief in the reality of sin, although within the dream we can *believe* it can.

CLARKE: It is not constrained. That's fine with regard to the inner divine life and our own life in heaven, united with God. But down in this life we are not yet in heaven, but must make moral choices to get there, to respond to the call of God to awaken from the dream, etc. Here we need free choice.

WAPNICK: Again, the Course would agree with respect to life in Heaven. The will of God's Son is not constrained in the sense of there not being anything but the Will of God and Christ, which are one. And so nothing exists that could constrain, restrict, or change it. There is no ego in Heaven, no thought of opposite or limitation. In fact, there is no thought at all. Heaven is, again, a non-dualistic state of perfect oneness. But within the dream, as I said just before, *A Course in Miracles* does very much talk about freedom to choose. And in that sense, the traditional notion of free will would apply, definitely. On that level, our freedom to choose is between, as I mentioned right at the beginning, listening to the Voice of the Holy Spirit, which would always be a Voice of joining, forgiveness, love, and peace, as opposed to the choice to hear the voice of the ego, which would always tell us to attack, condemn, feel guilty, judge, have conflict, etc.

On that level of the dream, therefore, there is definitely a freedom. The appeal of the Course to us is really on that level. Nonetheless, it needs to be clearly understood that this belief in free will or choice within the level of the dream—even between the ego and the Holy Spirit—is still illusory, and therefore cannot constitute a *real* choice since, once again, in reality there is no choice. And needless to say, the world's notion of choosing between illusions in terms of personal satisfaction is clearly no choice at all, since God is omitted from either alternative.

One of the things *A Course in Miracles* teaches repeatedly—in fact the very last section of the text is entitled "Choose Once Again"—is that we should always make another choice: where before we had chosen to hear the voice of the ego and to make separation real, to live out that separation with ourselves here in this world, we now can make another choice to hear the Voice of forgiveness. So where we saw the world as a place in which we could attack God and hide from Him, we now can see the world as a classroom in which we learn the meaning of joining. And the joining that we do in this world, which is a joining in forgiveness—a joining in sharing a common purpose—then becomes the mirror or reflection of what the Course calls "the greater joining," which is our joining as Christ with God.

CLARKE: But then my difficulty would be: Who is doing this choosing? Choosing is a very personal act and a very real act. And if this is all a dream, it would seem there is nobody who is doing the choosing. There is no real person doing the choosing, because a dream is an unreal state. So we have a kind of unreal chooser making a kind of unreal choice. I don't see how real freedom could be there and how the Holy Spirit could be appealing to us, because there is no "I" which could be making this act of choice one way or the other—because this "I" would be something distinct from God, a distinct center, joined with God indeed, but it would still be a distinct center which is capable of making its own actions. Otherwise it is an unreal choice, it would seem.

WAPNICK: You are quite correct, Norris; basically it is an unreal freedom. It is an illusory freedom. At this point, let me comment briefly on the nature of the ego, or the false self. Choice, as I was saying, has meaning only within the level of the dream. And the dream we call the world is the home of the ego. *A Course in Miracles* defines "ego" as the thought system of the separation, or the separated self. So it has much more in common with the Eastern notions of a false self than with Freud's psychoanalytic ego. The ego is the thought of separation taken seriously, believed as real and called *sin*. This then leads to our constructing defenses to protect ourselves from our belief in *guilt* over separating from God, and finally our *fear* of God's retaliation, all of which are an integral part of the ego system. And, briefly stated, these defenses are denial and projection, the devices used by the ego to convince us that *we* are not the sinful and guilty ones, but that someone else is.

We could look at this false self as essentially consisting of three thoughts—sin, guilt, and fear—which I think is a way of answering your question, Norris. There is, however, a part of our split minds that chooses to hear the voice of this false self. And I think part of the confusion stems from the Course's frequent use of the word "ego" to denote *only* that voice of attack, hatred, separation, and guilt. In a larger sense, however, the word "ego" can also be understood to be the entire false self or split mind, which again has three parts.

The first part of the false self would be that voice of hatred and separation, what the Course also refers to as the wrong mind. The second part would be the part of our minds, the right mind, that hears the Voice of the Holy Spirit, which speaks of joining, forgiveness, and peace. And then there is a third part of our minds that has to choose between these two, what I have referred to as the decision maker. It is this part of our split minds that the Course is truly directed at: that part that can choose between these two contradictory thought systems: a thought system of separation, hatred, and death; and a thought system of forgiveness, love, and unity.

CLARKE: It would have to be a very real part of the mind, though, it seems.

WAPNICK: The Course would say no, it is not a real part of the mind, which I think is where our difference enters in. See, again, the real part of our mind is the capital "S" Self, or our Christ Mind. That part does not choose. That part is still at home with God, is still at one with the Father. So the part that we are talking about is the part that seemed to fall asleep, that seemed to split off from God—that part is the realm of choice. So, in a sense, freedom is illusory, as you were pointing out. In other words, the dream begins with our making the wrong choice: choosing to listen to the wrong voice, and then identifying with that voice of separation. Therefore, within the dream, before we can awaken from the dream, we have to allow that faulty voice to be corrected by the Holy Spirit.

CLARKE: From inside the dream.

WAPNICK: From inside the dream, exactly. That is the role of the Holy Spirit. One of the concepts that the Course talks about is "the happy dream." The happy dream is the Holy Spirit's teachings of forgiveness, the corrections for the ego's nightmare dreams. But the happy dream still remains illusory, because we are correcting what ultimately never happened

68

(as understood within the Course's system). The part of our mind that chooses between these two dreams, the nightmare dream of the ego, and the happy dream of forgiveness of the Holy Spirit, is the third part of our mind, the decision maker. But this is all within the illusory self.

CLARKE: That would be difficult—to think of that very important part that is going to make the choice for the Holy Spirit, as not being really real.

WAPNICK: Yes, absolutely—which is why I talk about Level One and Level Two. Level Two speaks to us only within the dream where we believe we are, and here we do feel that we always have a choice. If something happens to me in my waking life that I don't like, I have a choice whether to get angry and attack, or to forgive. That choice is very real to me, within the dream. And obviously, I am aware that I could choose A or B, the ego or the Holy Spirit; so there must be a third part of my mind, again, that can choose A or B. *A Course in Miracles* speaks to me within this dream, and talks about the Holy Spirit as being that memory of God that extends into the dream. Or, as I like to think of it, the Holy Spirit is that part of the mind that, while it fell asleep, still has a memory of what Heaven was like, so the Holy Spirit is like a memory in my dreaming mind of that perfect Love of God, and that memory connects me back to the truth of my Identity as Christ.

CLARKE: The Holy Spirit, though, would not exactly be divine itself, like the Third Person of the Christian Trinity, but rather the memory of my state of union with God.

WAPNICK: Yes, it is like a function, you see; so the Course's use of "Holy Spirit" would be different from the traditional Trinitarian concept. It is like a function, a memory of God's Love that I took into the dream with me. When I fell asleep, I carried that memory with me.

CLARKE: Now, Kenneth, that is remarkably similar to the Neoplatonic doctrine of Plotinus. We mentioned Plotinus before; he was a brilliant man, the great founder in the third century of the Neoplatonic school that was an improvement over Plato.

WAPNICK: He is a great love of yours, I know.

CLARKE: Yes, and a great influence on Christianity, but, still, he was very opposed to Christianity. He says that when the soul falls down into the body, as into a kind of prison, the soul never totally falls. He believes that there is a higher part of the soul that is always in union with the One, but that there is a lower part, inhabited by the "self" of human consciousness, that can sink to lower levels of being according to what we choose to love. It can thus get stuck in the body, but can also respond to the call of the Good and rise again to its higher level, like a "traveler" on the scale of being, becoming like what it loves.

WAPNICK: And, as I recall, he does speak very movingly in some passages of this call to the soul.

CLARKE: The notion of two levels of consciousness of self is also quite prominent in the Vedanta. Just recently I was speaking with a famous Indian philosopher. He was speaking about living consciously down in this world, which is real for our purposes here, where you really have moral responsibility and you have to meet your obligations—a whole world of things that are very important in this world of secondary reality. It's very real, very important; you have a whole set of moral obligations, and duties in life, and so on. But then, when you get in the higher state, all that multiplicity somehow drops off. So there are two levels of the same being. They don't quite speak of it as a dream exactly. Some will speak of it as a kind of illusion. Others will say it's impossible to understand. But once you are in the upper level, then all the multiplicity disappears. Perhaps the Course's view is similar to that.

WAPNICK: Yes, it is very similar. And *A Course in Miracles* would basically say the same thing you are saying. When the collective dream is over—what the Course refers to as the Second Coming and Last Judgment—all memory of the dream is gone, disappearing back into its own inherent nothingness.

CLARKE: Of course, as I have been saying, a Christian would have great trouble with the notion that God does not know everything that is going on, even a dream...

WAPNICK: A lot of students of the Course have the same trouble...

CLARKE: ...since God is the sustainer of all being, even of the one that's thinking and everything that we think or dream. Even a dream isn't just simply nothingness. It is the activity of a real dreamer. Hence to think of something going on that God doesn't know and isn't somehow supporting and cooperating with would be a very difficult notion of God for me to make sense out of—that God is not really the sustainer of all being, and doesn't know what we know, i.e., our dreaming. That would be implying limitation on God. It would seem to us that He should know that, with compassion, and try to bring us back to reality. It is not a limitation to *know* the imperfect, but only to *be* it.

WAPNICK: The interesting thing about your statement— that God's not knowing about the dream places a limitation on Him—is that it is used by *A Course in Miracles* as proof of its own position. The Course would say that even knowing about this imperfect world, let alone interacting with it, would limit God by stating that imperfection actually exists, reflecting that the impossible has happened. This would support the ego's belief that it has successfully placed a limit on God by "creating" something outside perfect oneness. This once again highlights the differences between *A Course in Miracles* and Christianity. We always come back to that basic metaphysical distinction. *A Course in Miracles*, after all, is a perfect, non-dualistic system. There is nothing outside totality, wholeness, the everything, or in St. Paul's wonderful phrase, God is All in All, which Jesus quotes a few times in the Course. Therefore, again, how could the perfect God know about an illusory imperfect world?

CLARKE: Yes. Now, on that level of living down in this world, I think the notion of ego—which we haven't had enough chance really to develop—the notion of ego constantly using excuses, the body for example, to flee from God and project blame onto others, is a very rich psychological insight. That is really one of the things I like a great deal, as you know, about the Course—despite my trouble with the origins of it. But it would seem to me, at least for the Christian, that it is very important for a person to admit his or her own guilt first; that "I made a choice, it was a bad choice, and I could have done better." It was not just "Oh, I didn't know any better, it was just ignorance, so I'm not responsible." We are to take responsibility, as in the Old Testament account of David stealing Uriah's wife, Bathsheba (2 Sam 11-12). He had Uriah sent to war where he was killed, and then David takes his wife. Samuel accuses him, and David says "I have sinned before God." There was no business about "the subconscious did me in," or "somebody was trying to persecute me," or "the environment was poor." He says "*I* have sinned before God." Taking responsibility for one's sins, then, should not really oppress one with guilt, because once one has done that before God, then God forgives it and it is gone. You should not go back on it. But you have that sense of humbly being a forgiven sinner with a new kind of love. The idea is to take responsibility for one's own sin, but not to be burdened with this terrible, constant burden of guilt. To admit your guilt and then ask forgiveness would be an important difference.

WAPNICK: The Course would actually agree with you on that, Norris. The difference is that *A Course in Miracles* does not see the process of looking at one's guilt and accepting responsibility for it as having to do with God, as such.

Frequently, the Course is misunderstood by its own students, which is what led me many years ago to start talking about Level One and Level Two, since the Course's metaphysical teachings are often confused with its practical teachings. So very often people have misinterpreted *A Course in Miracles* to mean that since it says that there is no guilt and all this is a dream, then I can do whatever I want and I am not responsible for it. Or if I am responsible, it is all an illusion anyway so it doesn't matter what I do, etc. Many people have, unfortunately, done in some fashion what David did, and then justified it on the grounds that this is all a dream anyway, so what difference does it make? That would be the farthest you could get from the real teaching and spirit of *A Course in Miracles*.

The Course would say, using David as an example, that what would be truly healing and responsible would be for someone to recognize—having stolen another man's wife, and then seeing to it that that man was placed in the front lines of battle so that he would be killed and gotten out of the way—that the real cause of his actions was his desire to keep the separation real; to keep himself so guilty that the Love of God would be blocked in his mind, or that he would not be aware of the Love of God that was already present in his mind. And finally, still using David as an example, that his pretense of being innocent was being totally irresponsible to Uriah, himself, and to God.

CLARKE: Also to think that he needs to be filled up because he is empty.

WAPNICK: Absolutely right, yes; that really goes to the core of the Course's teaching on special relationships. See, you are quite a student of the Course yourself.

CLARKE: Well that's the good part of the Course.

WAPNICK: Actually, the dynamic of the special relationship is crucial to the thought system of the Course, as I mentioned earlier: that we feel we are lacking something within ourselves; that we have banished God from our minds entirely and so there is a big hole. Then we have to fill up that hole by taking things—stealing things—from the outside. *A Course in Miracles* explains that that never works because it still does not change the basic premise, which is the belief that I have lost the Love of God and lost my Identity as God's child.

CLARKE: And actually there isn't anything that could fill that gap except God.

WAPNICK: Absolutely right, and *A Course in Miracles* is very clear about that. It says at one point that the only real relationship we have is our relationship with God. And what we do is use other relationships as ways of substituting for that. So that...

CLARKE: ...or you could use them as positive ways to express that: for example, a loving relationship.

WAPNICK: Yes, or you could really join with someone not in the sense of trying to possess, cannibalize, or attack them, but to really join with the Christ in another, which is mirroring the Christ in you. This joining really means accepting the joining that is *already* present in the relationship. The Course would call this a "holy relationship," the process of shifting the relationship's purpose from one of separation and guilt to one of joining and expressing the Love of God...

CLARKE: ... or to fill up a need.

WAPNICK: Yes, and the only real need we have is to remember that we have no needs because we remain as God created us. That is one of the Course's major principles.

CLARKE: Could you go back now to the case of David and how the Course explains that?

WAPNICK: Yes, so what *A Course in Miracles* would say to David to begin with is just what *you* are saying: that you believed you had a need that could only be met by stealing another man's wife. What *A Course in Miracles* would say on a deeper level is that David was reenacting his belief that he had stolen from God, because that is basically what the ego thought system begins with. It begins with the belief that God has something I do not have; namely, that He is the prime Creator. The ego wants to steal that from Him and usurp His role as the prime Creator or First Cause. Then the ego feels guilty for that sin of stealing from God. That is the beginning of the fall, from the Course's point of view: the guilt over *believing* we have stolen from God, and then the fear that God is going to come raging after us and steal back from us the power we stole from Him. And then He would destroy us. *A Course in Miracles* then sees the world—to return briefly to this important point—as the place in which we hide from God. That is the Course's view of the world.

So deep within us is that horrifying thought: "I have stolen from God." And what we all do is what in another context Freud described as the "repetition compulsion": We are compelled to repeat our sins over and over again. So I think that on the ultimate level, David's stealing of Uriah's wife Bathsheba was really his way of reenacting the theft from Heaven, stealing from God. And, again, what does David then do? He positions Uriah to get killed in battle, which is the expression of the ego's belief that it has destroyed God so that it could have its way and keep what it stole. This is the ego's ultimate guilt.

So to come back again to the message of Jesus and the crucifixion: in effect, Jesus acts God out for us, and then tells us: "You believe you have killed God, both in that ontological instant and then on Calvary, but the truth is nothing happened. My love for you has not changed, just as God's Love for you has not changed." Therefore, I think that what David was doing in that wonderful biblical story was acting out for all of us that theft from God and the murder of God. The reason David is such a popular figure is that he is so human for all of us; he has all the ego foibles that people share. And so everyone can so easily identify with him.

And so A Course in Miracles would say to David: "Look at what you have done and accept responsibility for it. But what you have done—on the bodily level—is simply a symbol. As real as it seems within the dream, it is but a symbol of your deeper belief in the sin of having stolen from God. And what you have to do now is bring your guilt to the Love of the Holy Spirit in your mind. This is the Love you have sought to avoid through your attraction to specialness—love for Bathsheba, and hate for Uriah—and it is this substitution for God that your actions represent, this decision for specialness that you are responsible for and which must be undone."

In this sense the Course's answer would not be really different, I think, from what Christianity would teach. What A Course in Miracles says is that you bring your illusion to the truth, or the darkness to the light. And once you do that, then the light of God's Love that is present in our minds, which is what the Course calls the Holy Spirit, dissolves all that darkness. But that cannot happen if we maintain our belief that we are justified in what we have done, or attempt to spiritualize our mistakes.

CLARKE: Yes, but then wouldn't he have to admit that that was a wrong choice and he didn't have to do it, in the sense that he did it freely? Wouldn't he have to say, "I didn't have to act this out and I'm sorry for that"?

WAPNICK: Yes, of course. I think that what you refer to is what many Christians today call "healthy guilt." *A Course in Miracles* would agree with that, but would use a different term. It would certainly talk about the need and responsibility to look within one's mind at one's choices to "sin," to separate, to attack. My guilt—or self hatred—would then tell me that I have done something wrong, which may lead to various symptoms: I do not feel right, I am not sleeping well, not eating well; there is anxiety, depression; something is very wrong. And the Course would tell me that what is wrong is not that I have sinned, but that I have made a wrong choice, and I now must bring that wrong choice to the Love of the Holy Spirit or Jesus Who can help me to accept the correct choice They already hold out for me. What is required for that to occur is what *A Course in Miracles* calls "the little willingness" to look at our mistakes and bring them to the Love of God. So I think in that sense we would probably agree.

CLARKE: Yes that's fine, that's much closer, but David would have to say, "I did that freely, I was not compelled to do that."

WAPNICK: Absolutely, he would have to take full responsibility for his dream of lust, jealousy, and ultimately murder, and realize that "the devil didn't make me do it," but that it was his own choice.

CLARKE: Yes, "the devil didn't make me do it and it wasn't just my unconscious dreaming; no, I was enough responsible so I'm sorry now, and I wish I hadn't done that." Saying "I'm sorry" would be saying again that something is real, at least inside the dream. It isn't saying, "Oh no, I never did that at all," or "I just couldn't help doing that." No, it is saying that "I take responsibility."

WAPNICK: Well, the Course is very clear about this. It stresses the power of our mind to choose, within the dream. The ultimate point is that no matter what we have chosen to dream here and make real, it has had no effect on our reality as God's child, and has never really separated us from God. But within the dream it most definitely has had what appear to be, and what we experience as, real effects, and those have to be looked at.

CLARKE: Kenneth, reflecting on this part of our discussion, it does seem to me, looking in from the outside, that what the Course calls the "dream world" actually has considerably more density, drama, moral urgency, coherence of cause and effect, and hence approximation to reality than is meant when we speak in ordinary language of a "dream state," so that the term in the Course seems to approximate what might be called a metaphor or symbol for a mysterious state beyond our power of description. And the Course does say we can be sorry for what we experience as the real effects of our mistaken choices, doesn't it?

WAPNICK: Oh, yes. Again, we are asked to accept responsibility for everything we experience and for everything we do. We are not the innocent victims of the world. It is our dream. And you are quite right, Norris; while the dynamics of our sleeping and waking dreams are the same, it is so much easier to experience the unreality of our sleeping dreams than the basic unreality of our waking experience. And so, *A Course in Miracles* does not ask us to use metaphysics as a way of excusing ego choices to hurt others.

CLARKE: That is an important point because when you say that forgiveness means that you see the sin was not real, you are referring to this other level...

WAPNICK: ...the ontological level, or the metaphysical level, yes.

CLARKE: But you can't get to that level, really, until you do take responsibility down in this realm.

WAPNICK: Yes, and that really is important...

CLARKE: Yes, that is very important because it is frequently misunderstood or misrepresented by people who say, "Now I can get rid of all my guilt," or "I never really sinned," by which they mean down inside the world of the dream they never did anything wrong. But that is not what you are saying.

WAPNICK: No, *A Course in Miracles* is quite clear about that. Again, that line I referred to earlier says: "You are not guiltless in time, but in eternity." Within the dream we made guilt real. God does not see us that way, but within our belief system we are definitely guilty and we have to accept responsibility for that. It was not an abstract ego that did it, it was not the devil that did it, it was my choice. And I must look at that choice with openness and honesty and see what I have done to attack another person, to attack myself, to attack God, and bring that wrong choice to the Love of the Holy Spirit. Jesus is quite emphatic in the Course that we are not to deny our physical experience in the world, and moreover, that it is almost an impossibility to do so. He is not encouraging denial or repression. As I explained earlier, to deny one's guilt and hatred is to ensure that it will be projected out in the form of attack—either onto one's body or onto others.

CLARKE: But it is not really a sin against God, because for him it is not really real.

WAPNICK: That's right; God does not hold it against me. There is a line in the Course—in fact the line is repeated—which says "God does not forgive because He has never condemned" (workbook, pp. 73,79; W-pI.46:1:1; W-pI.60.1:2). God simply loves. But the problem is *we* do not love. And so we have made up a world and a thought system of hate and attack.

CLARKE: In the Christian perspective we would say that we really have sinned against God, by breaking or wounding a personal bond of loving obedience, and that God knows this. But this makes no change in him; it does not threaten or diminish him in any way. His love always remains the same, enveloping us on all sides; we are the ones who let it in or keep it out. As I said earlier, St. Thomas says that God is offended by sin not because it hurts *him*, but only because it hurts *us*, and he does not want his children to be hurt. And as soon as we repent, his compassionate, forgiving love pours into us again and our relation with him is healed; he bears no grudges, or resentment. Our sins hurt only ourselves, not him. So on this point our thought systems actually come closer.

WAPNICK: Yes, with that latter statement especially, that our choices have hurt us. And we cannot deny that, nor theologize nor "metaphysicalize" that away—if that is a word—but we must look at what we have done, the choices we have made here, and change them here. So in that sense *A Course in Miracles* does urge its students to take a deep responsibility, not only for what they do, but even more importantly for what they think. It is teaching us that it is our thinking that affects what we do. Thus, we really have to change the underlying thought system, and we cannot do it without accepting the Love of the Holy Spirit within us. But the essential difference here, to restate this important point, is that in *A Course in Miracles* God does not even know "we have done it," because in truth we haven't.

CLARKE: Fine; our differences here are clear. Now one last point about this dream state we are in at present. It would seem, from what I have read here and there about the Course, that this present world is really only a projection of our thoughts, e.g., the weather, disease, suffering, depression and other psychological disorders, death, etc. It would seem to follow then that by changing our thoughts we could do away at will with all these evils. Now I understand you to say, a bit earlier, that our individual egos are part of a larger ego system that originally broke off from God and then fragmented, so that we as individuals cannot change the world by changing our thoughts. Could you explain how that works in the Course, and whether or not we can change the world by changing our thoughts about it? In a Christian world, of course, we could not do this, since the material world is a real world created by God and operating under his laws and providence, interacting with us but not dependent for its being on us.

WAPNICK: In principle, I think we could—since we are all of one mind, and the world has come from that mind. Appearances and experience to the contrary, there is after all only one Son and one dream. And the world and the mind that dreamt it are one; cause and effect are together. And so there is no world outside the Son's mind that believes in it.

In practice, though, I quite agree with you. And *A Course in Miracles* would, too. In practice, it is all that we can do to maintain some control over our individual minds and our individual thoughts: thoughts of separation, anger, sadness, loss, depression, etc. We are all so identified with that particular thought system of the ego that that is what the focus is: it is really not to move a mountain, or raise someone from the

81

dead, or change weather patterns. Again, since this is all occurring within the dream, we could *in principle* at any given point simply awaken from the dream, or even change things in the dream, just as we can so easily change television channels. However, in practice it is not like that at all. In practice, the constant focus of the Course is to help us look at our thoughts, not so that we could change our thoughts about the weather or other physical things in the world, but so that through the Holy Spirit's help we could change our thoughts of guilt to thoughts of forgiveness. As the Course says: "Seek not to change the world, but choose to change your mind about the world" (text, p. 415; T-21.in.1:7).

CLARKE: But if there is a larger kind of ego mind that is producing all of this, is that ego mind also going to get a kind of redemption, a kind of enlightenment, and this whole thing will disappear?

WAPNICK: Eventually, as individual minds here join within the dream of time, there will be what *A Course in Miracles* calls the Second Coming. The Course reinterprets the traditional notion of the Second Coming to mean the time when the whole mind of the Sonship is healed, the entire fragmentary process has been reversed, and the split mind of the Sonship is restored to its original unity. This is at the very end of time; and again, that is not the focus of *A Course in Miracles*. But that is the Course's definition of the Second Coming of Christ, and has nothing to do with Jesus. It is the awakening of the Son from the dream. That occurs at the very end point of a much larger process, which *A Course in Miracles* says will occur over millions of years. But the focus is really on the individual process of awakening.

SUMMARY AND CONCLUSIONS

CLARKE: I think we have now covered the main points of disagreement between the Course and Christianity, as the two of us see it, and the time has now come to move toward a conclusion. Let me gather together into a condensed summary just how these differences work out.

1) Christianity believes that God *created this material world*, out of nothing preexisting, that it is imperfect but still an image of God and basically *good*, and a theater for our moral and spiritual growth toward the full stature of sons and daughters of God on pilgrimage toward final blissful union with God in transformed or "glorified" bodies in Heaven. The Course believes this material world is not the product of God at all, but of part of the original Christ consciousness that broke off in a kind of dream of separation from God (not a real separation) and produced this material world as a kind of dream world or thought projection as an expression of the ego's attempt to escape from God. God does not even know of the existence of this "dream world" because it is in fact unreal.

2) For Christianity, Jesus is the *Son of God*, Second Person of the Triune God, hence possessing the same *divine nature* as his Father, who has freely taken on a real body and human nature, born of Mary, walked the human journey in a body in this material world in order to show us how to live as authentic children of God, really died on the cross to atone for our sins, and rose again in a real but glorified body to dwell as such forever with his Father and the Holy Spirit in Heaven. The Course believes that Jesus is not really divine in nature, but is part of the original Christ consciousness that tried to break off from God to create the dream world we are living in now, but was the first one to wake up from this dream and recognize it as such, and is now a loving teacher who helps

83

the rest of us wake up, too. Hence he has no real body, nor did he therefore really die on the cross nor rise from the dead holding on to a real body forever. All this is only part of the dream world of thought projection of the ego as separated from God.

3) According to Christianity, Jesus *really died on the cross* to atone for human sins, to teach us both the depth of evil in serious sin and the even greater depth of divine love as willing to forgive us and restore us to an even higher union with God. He *rose from the dead* in a *real but glorified body* to carry out effectively this restoration of us to an even closer union with God than we had before our sins. The Course, on the other hand, teaches that Jesus never really died on the cross; his "dream" body was indeed put on the cross but only appeared to die according to the thought projection of those who wished to put him to death and so get rid of him and of God in the process. He therefore did not really rise in a real body, which was never real in the first place. The Gospel account is just symbolic of the remembrance of Jesus by his disciples.

4) According to Christian teaching, the *Eucharist* is the sacrament of the transformation of bread and wine into the real body and blood of Christ, veiled under the appearances of bread and wine, which is the endlessly repeated memorial of the death of Jesus for our sins that takes place in the Catholic Mass or Eucharistic liturgy. For the Course, there cannot be any such real transformation of bread and wine into the body and blood of Jesus, because he never had such a real body in the first place. It is only a memorial, therefore, of the love of Jesus for us.

5) According to the Course, the *nature of the dream world* we are now living in is that it does not represent a genuine reality but only a thought projection of an apparent separation from God from which arose our illusory ego and its weaving of this dream of a material world separate from God as an escape of the ego from its dream of the pursuing vengeance

of God. This dream world was not produced by our present individual egos, but by one original ego which broke off in its thought world and then progressively fragmented into the multiple egos we experience as individual human beings today. But once in this dream world, we have to live in it and cope with it in a morally responsible and loving, forgiving way, as Jesus taught us, so that we may wake up from the dream as soon as the lesson of our schooling in this "classroom" is completed, and turn back again to the blissful union with God we never really lost. Christian thinkers object to the idea that we never really sinned or turned away from God, and that in a dream world we could have the necessary free will to make genuine moral decisions or decide to return to God. They fear the reality and central importance of the moral world would disappear, since only real persons, they believe, can make authentic moral decisions.

WAPNICK: Well, I think again we are quite in agreement over these main points, but I would like to restate some of the points you made regarding the Course, especially in relation to the position of Christianity.

To begin with, *A Course in Miracles* would certainly disagree that the "final blissful union with God" occurs in a transformed or "glorified" body. Its position, as we have seen, is that bodies keep us separate and in a state unlike our true Identity as spirit and Christ, God's one Son. Therefore, you would never find a dichotomy such as St. Paul made between God's only Son, Jesus, and the rest of us, God's adopted sons.

Regarding Jesus, *A Course in Miracles* would not deny that Jesus is divine, as long as it is understood that so is everyone else as Christ, and that ontologically there is no difference between us. However, it is also the case that in Christ there is no individuality. God's one Son has but one name: Christ. The Course would also not speak of Jesus as having been part of the "original Christ consciousness that tried to

85

break off from God," etc. Again, to speak in such a manner gives the separation a reality the Course emphatically states never happened. Nor would it even use the word "consciousness" to describe the state of Christ, since that is an inherently dualistic term that belies the non-dualistic unity of Heaven.

Coming to the crucifixion of Jesus, I would like to add to your comments, Norris. The Jesus of *A Course in Miracles* was demonstrating the inherent falsity of the unconscious thought we hold that we have killed God and His Love. By allowing the dreamers of the world's dream—the separated ones—to act out in form their unconscious belief of murdering God and crucifying His Son, Jesus demonstrated: 1) the body is not our reality; 2) God, His Son, and Their Love cannot be destroyed; and 3) the dream of death had no effect on him, since he was not asleep, and therefore invulnerable to the attack thoughts and behavior within the dream. As I said before, the Course states that the message of the crucifixion is: "Teach only love, for that is what you are."

One more point about Jesus and the Gospels: Since the biblical account of Jesus is so discrepant from the one in the Course, one could not truly say, as you did, that according to the Course "the Gospel account is just symbolic of the remembrance of Jesus by his disciples." I am reminded of something you said to me many years ago, Norris. After hearing me state that the Course came as a correction to Christianity, you commented, and quite accurately, that when you correct something you retain the basic framework of the original. But *A Course in Miracles* retains nothing of the original framework of Christianity. And the same could just as truly be said about the Course and the biblical account of Jesus' life, death, and resurrection.

Similarly regarding the doctrine of the Eucharist: As we have seen, there are at least two passages in the Course that specifically refute the Church's teachings about Jesus' desire to share his body with his followers. However, like anything else of the ego's world, the ritual of communion could be used by the Holy Spirit to serve a different purpose—in this case, as a reminder that Jesus came to share his mind with us, not his body. But in and of itself, the sacrament has no meaning apart from this general purpose of forgiveness.

Finally, while *A Course in Miracles* would not really use the term "morally responsible" as it is commonly used in our society, it certainly would encourage its students to live in a loving and forgiving way, as you mentioned. Moreover, as we have discussed, the Course quite emphatically encourages its students to be responsible, *but on a much deeper level*. As students of *A Course in Miracles*, we are asked to be totally responsible for *all* our thoughts, which come from our mind's decision to join with the ego or with Jesus. From that decision come our beliefs, feelings, and behavior. If this underlying decision is not changed from the ego to the Holy Spirit—from the wrong to the right mind—then simply modifying behavior will never heal. And in the long run this would reinforce a lack of responsibility on all levels of our experience—as is witnessed by the history of this planet—since we had not assumed the primary responsibility for our original decision to be separate from the Love of God.

To make the point still once again, the essential characteristic of *A Course in Miracles* that lies at the core of the differences you have nicely summarized is that it is a non-dualistic spirituality. Christianity, as Judaism before it, is a dualistic thought system in which God and the world, spirit and matter, co-exist as separate states, both of which are real. Reality is thus seen to be a dimension of opposites—as with good and evil—in marked distinction from the Course's understanding of reality as being only perfect unity in which there are no opposites.

But we certainly, once again, agree that it is not helpful for people, whether they are students of the Course, Roman Catholics, Protestants, Hindus, or whatever their spiritual path, to confuse the different paths. As was mentioned right at the beginning, the Course says it is only one path among many thousands.

CLARKE: You are very honest and forthright about that, and I admire this very much. In fact, you are the one who invited me to share this dialogue with you, in order to make perfectly clear to people interested in the Course the *differences* between it and traditional Christianity, that the two are not compatible. You asked me to state the differences clearly and strongly, not gloss them over. One of the difficulties, as the Course moves around and spreads its influence, is that not a few people, including some Catholic priests and nuns, do tend to gloss over these differences or try to combine things from both or assimilate the Course into Christianity because both speak of Jesus. This ends up causing considerable confusion, I regret to say.

WAPNICK: It is very confusing. What it ends up doing is watering down both the richness of the Christian tradition as well as the richness of *A Course in Miracles*. And I agree with you, that it is much more honest to say that these are the differences, and that if this is the path that brings me closer to God, then this is the path I will follow; and if another path does the same thing, then that is the path I should follow.

CLARKE: Yes, I have no difficulty in people following different paths, as long as they do it sincerely, honestly...

WAPNICK: I know you don't. That's unusual, you know.

CLARKE: I have seen so many people who have followed different paths with great fruit, East and West. I have known many such wonderful people in the Eastern tradition.

WAPNICK: There is a line in the Course, actually, that states: "A universal theology is impossible, but a universal

88

experience is not only possible but necessary" (manual, p. 73; C-in.2:5). And that universal experience would be the experience of the Love of God.

CLARKE: Well said!

WAPNICK: I think that because we are so fragmented, so separate, and so different, that to reach the goal of having that universal experience we each need different spiritual paths. And that in the end, one path is not any better than any other. In the end, in fact, all paths disappear into the Love of God.

CLARKE: Well, one could argue whether one is better than the other.

WAPNICK: That is another dialogue...

CLARKE: With respect to this point of not confusing different paths, let me ask you a practical question which has me a bit puzzled. I feel there are a number of particular spiritual and psychological insights from the practical level of the Course, such as I mentioned earlier, that can be used with profit by all religious people, including Christians. But it seems that many teachers of the Course throughout the country, and elsewhere, focus just on the practical teachings on this level and omit, almost entirely, mention of the deeper metaphysical and theological teachings of Level One—the dream and its origins, etc. This, too, can cause confusion for some Christians. So may I ask you what you think of this practice, whether it is sound practice in the true spirit of the Course to teach Level Two without the background and foundation of Level One, in a word, to separate the practice from the theory. Is this legitimate and wise to try to help people this way?

WAPNICK: No, not in my opinion. There are many other spiritualities that would teach, as does *A Course in Miracles*, that forgiveness is to be preferred to holding grievances, that developing a relationship with Jesus or the Holy Spirit is essential to our return home, that God loves us and does not seek to destroy us, etc. However, there is no other spirituality that I am aware of that combines a non-dualistic metaphysics with the very sophisticated psychology one finds in the Course. And one that places the meaning of forgiveness in the context of this non-dualistic metaphysics. When one removes this context from the teaching of forgiveness, one has truly lost the meaning Jesus has given it in the Course—which is, once again, that in the end there is nothing to forgive because nothing happened to disturb the peace and love that *is* God's Son. And so at the point that one has removed the concept of forgiveness from the Course's metaphysics, one has taken away the very heart of *A Course in Miracles*—its non-duality. And one then can no longer be said to be speaking about *A Course in Miracles* at all, but rather some other spiritual path that is dualistic. And again, it is a disservice to everyone to misrepresent the Course that way.

CLARKE: Let me conclude now by suggesting that despite all our differences, we can work together in our own ways toward healing one of the great illusions of the modern secularist world: the belief that we are empty in ourselves (partly true) but that the way to fill up this emptiness is by filling it with creatures, with what is not of God. There is a great restlessness and sense of inner emptiness in so much of the modern world, together with the illusion of consumerism, that somehow possessing and consuming more and more material goods will assuage this restlessness and fill this emptiness, always with something other than and less than God himself. But the more material possessions we gather, the poorer we seem to get interiorly. As St. Augustine noted with great insight long ago, forgetting our own interior spiritual riches, we think we are poor, and go begging outside ourselves among material things seeking to become rich, but in the process become poorer and poorer, since the lower cannot satisfy the higher. This illusion of paradise without God is a profound illusion indeed.

WAPNICK: I think that we would both agree, certainly, that no love is possible in this world without its Source being God. And the whole idea of *A Course in Miracles* is to help us bring to the Holy Spirit all of the ego's interferences to love that are in our minds—i.e., switch to our right minds, where at last we can become an instrument of the Holy Spirit. His Love then can extend through us and so, in this world, we do become more peaceful and more loving to ourselves and to each other. There is a beautiful passage in the workbook where Jesus says:

> For this alone I need; that you will hear the words I speak, and give them to the world. You are my voice, my eyes, my feet, my hands through which I save the world (workbook, p. 322; W-pI.rV.9:2-3).

CLARKE: In one of the articles I wrote, "What It Means To Be a Person," based on the thought of St. Thomas Aquinas, I gave three stages: *self-possession* through self-awareness and self-governing of your actions; then *self-communication*; finally *self-transcendence*, where you go out of your own limited point of view to take on the point of view of the Mind and the Will of God, to see the whole world as God sees it, and then to love all the good as God loves it in its proper order. That is a taking on of the very Mind and Love of God; that is a self-transcendence that then brings great joy. So to be yourself, you have to really step out of yourself—that limited self. It is not for the self to disappear entirely, I think, but it is to be fulfilled in taking something larger, the true Center, as one's own center.

WAPNICK: Yes, I think I might mention one other thing in view of what you just said, that the goal of *A Course in Miracles* is not really to be without a self, or to disappear from this world into the heart of God, as it says in one beautiful poetic passage. Its goal is to have us live without any guilt, without any sin, without any fear, without attack of any kind. That is the goal of the Course: to be present in this world, but to have all of our mistaken thoughts of judgment, hatred, fear, and guilt removed. And again, this is frequently misunderstood by students of the Course. As is said in John's Gospel, we are to live *in* the world, yet not be *of* it; i.e., live within the dream, but aware that we are not truly of it, and that our true Identity is outside the dream. In other words, we are to be in the world the way Jesus was.

CLARKE: But to live in this world as long as we are in it. So, there is a kind of death here, a kind of physical death.

WAPNICK: Yes, *A Course in Miracles* does not deny a physical death within the level of the dream. What it does say, actually, is that there are two kinds of death. There is the death that comes through guilt and fear, and the fear of judgment from the ego's projected image of God. And then there is the death which is described as a quiet laying down of the body when our work is done, recognizing that we have fulfilled the purpose of being here; namely, to have learned to be more loving and forgiving. And then our death is a peaceful one.

Another way of stating the goal of *A Course in Miracles* is that it is to live in this world in a peaceful way, not with all the conflict, both international as well as personal. And it does say, in fact, that knowledge—which is the Course's synonym for Heaven (actually a kind of Gnostic use of the word "knowledge")—is not the goal of this Course, peace is: the experience of peace here within the dream. It is a way of living with each other—both individually, as well as among nations—having the state of mind in which there is no conflict, no desire to usurp other people's place, and no need to steal what is not ours.

CLARKE: As Jesus said, I came that you might have peace; I came to give you my peace.

WAPNICK: The Jesus of *A Course in Miracles* would echo that too, certainly.

CLARKE: So we differ on much, but also agree on much. Let me give one last quotation from Charles Morgan, the novelist: "There is no surprise more magical than the surprise of being loved; it is God's finger on man's shoulder."

WAPNICK: That's wonderful. If I could add something relevant to that: *A Course in Miracles* would say that there is no greater joy in this world than the joy of knowing that one is forgiven, and that forgiveness can only come through experiencing the Love of God through Jesus or the Holy Spirit.

APPENDIX

GLOSSARY

atonement - usually, though not universally, defined in Christianity as the expiation of humanity's sins through the crucifixion and death of Jesus Christ, as willed by God—based upon the Old Testament tradition of atonement through sacrifice. In *A Course in Miracles*, it refers to the acceptance of the truth that the separation from God never really happened—and is always capitalized to distinguish it from the traditional Christian view.

creation - traditional Christianity: God created the world, which exists outside His being, and created human beings in His image; within the Trinity, the Son and Holy Spirit are regarded not as creations but as persons within one being, who "proceed" from the Father. *A Course in Miracles*: God creates only Christ by extending His being as spirit—a non-spatial extension; the physical world and the body are defined as the "miscreation" of the ego and have nothing to do with God; Christ is defined as God's Son of which we all are a part.

Crusades - Christian military expeditions from western Europe to recapture the Holy Land from the Moslems. They extended roughly from A.D. 1100 to A.D. 1300, and were characterized by particularly bloody aggressions, carried out in the name of Jesus and his Church.

Eucharist - in Christianity, the commemoration of the Last Supper described in the New Testament, when Jesus shared bread and wine with his disciples, calling the bread and wine his body and blood; one of seven sacraments in the Catholic Church, whereby the priest transforms bread and wine into the body and blood of Jesus Christ (the Real Presence of

Jesus), and then the priest and faithful partake of Jesus' body and blood in "holy communion."

Fathers of the Church - the theologians of the early Christian centuries, whose writings shaped Church theology and doctrine.

Gnosticism - a system of religious and philosophical theories and practices dating from the second century A.D. (some scholars trace its origins to earlier centuries); a movement later suppressed and declared heretical by the Church; in general, most Gnostics believed that the physical universe was not created by God, and therefore was inherently evil.

Inquisition - the organized effort on the part of the Roman Catholic Church to find and punish those it believed were heretics. It began in the 13th century with Pope Gregory IX, and continued on through the 16th century.

Neoplatonism - the extension of Platonism into the third century A.D. Plotinus was its foremost representative.

Plato (427-348 B.C.) - his major metaphysical teaching was that individual things in the world were imperfect reflections, or shadows, of their perfect, more real, abstract ideas which existed in a realm of their own. He regarded the body as a prison housing the soul, which longed to be liberated from its physical home.

Plotinus (205-270) - his thinking represented an advance over what Plato had begun; he defined an ultimate Source, called the One, from which everything emanated; as in Plato's system, the soul longed for its liberation from the physical world which imprisoned it.

St. Augustine (354-430) - a Father of the Church who attempted the integration of Christian teachings with the Platonic philosophical tradition.

St. Thomas Aquinas (1224-1274) - a leading philosopher and theologian whose thinking was highly influential in the Church and is expressed in the system of thought known as Thomism and neo-Thomism. He produced a unique synthesis of Platonic, Aristotelian, and Christian thought.

Vatican II - The meeting of the hierarchy of the Roman Catholic Church, convened by Pope John XXXIII between 1961 and 1965. It provided a more tolerant and contemporary framework for Church practice and the Church's relationship to other religions.

Vedanta - the strand of Hindu spirituality which expresses the non-dualistic nature of reality, known as Advaita Vedanta.

THE NICENE CREED

I believe in one God, the Father almighty, Maker of heaven and earth, and of all things visible and invisible. And in one Lord Jesus Christ, the only-begotten Son of God, born of the Father before all ages. God of God. Light of Light. True God of true God. Begotten, not made, consubstantial with the Father; by whom all things were made. Who for us men and for our salvation came down from heaven, and was incarnate by the Holy Spirit of the Virgin Mary; and was made man. He was also crucified for us, suffered under Pontius Pilate and was buried. And on the third day he arose again according to the Scriptures. He ascended into heaven, and sits at the right hand of the Father. And he shall come again with glory to judge the living and the dead; and of his kingdom there shall be no end. And in the Holy Spirit, the Lord and Giver of Life Who proceeds from the Father and the Son, Who together with the Father and the Son is adored and glorified, Who spoke through the Prophets. And in one, holy, Catholic and Apostolic Church. I confess one baptism for the remission of sins. And I look for the resurrection of the dead, and the life of the world to come. Amen.

KENNETH WAPNICK - BIOGRAPHICAL NOTE

Kenneth Wapnick was a close friend and associate of Helen Schucman and William Thetford, the two people whose joining together was the immediate stimulus for the scribing of *A Course in Miracles*. He is a clinical psychologist, having received his Ph.D. from Adelphi University in 1968, and is on the Executive Board of the Foundation for Inner Peace, publishers of *A Course in Miracles*. In 1982, Kenneth and his wife Gloria established the Foundation for *A Course in Miracles*, of which they are President and Vice-President. This Foundation is the teaching organization of the Foundation for Inner Peace. In 1988, they opened an Academy and Retreat Center in Roscoe, New York.

Kenneth is the author of twelve books on *A Course in Miracles*, one co-authored with Gloria, and is preparing other books for publication at the time of this writing. He also has authored several articles on *A Course in Miracles* and psychotherapy. In addition to conducting classes and workshops at the Foundation's Academy, he and Gloria have presented numerous lectures and workshops throughout the United States, as well as in Europe, Australia, and New Zealand. They publish a quarterly newsletter, "The Lighthouse."

A COURSE IN MIRACLES

How *A Course in Miracles* Came

A Course in Miracles was the result of a collaborative venture of two psychologists, Helen Schucman and William Thetford. They were, respectively, Associate and Full Professors of Medical Psychology at the Columbia-Presbyterian Medical Center in New York City. The Course came as a result of their joining together to find "another way" of relating to others, and began with Helen's "hearing" the inner voice of Jesus say to her one October evening in 1965: "This is a course in miracles. Please take notes."

Despite her considerable anxiety, Helen proceeded to take down in shorthand—over a seven-year period—the three books that comprise the Course. Helen's experience of Jesus' dictating voice was of an internal tape recorder that she could turn on or off at will. She did not go into a trance or altered state, or perform automatic writing. Helen was fully conscious and could be interrupted at any time, even in the middle of a sentence, and be able to return and pick up where she left off. Each day at the Medical Center, whenever time permitted in their very busy schedules, Helen would dictate to Bill what had been dictated to her the previous day, which Bill would then type out.

Much of *A Course in Miracles* is written in the first person, which is particularly relevant as Jesus refers many times to his crucifixion and resurrection, making it clear that from the perspective of his teachings in the Course, traditional Christianity had greatly misunderstood and distorted his message.

A Course in Miracles was published by the Foundation for Inner Peace in 1976, and at the time of the writing of this book (1994) has sold over one million copies worldwide.

Translations have been published in Spanish, Portuguese, and German, with other languages soon to follow.

Helen had difficulty applying the principles of *A Course in Miracles* to her life, though—contrary to the distorted accounts that have already begun to appear—she never doubted the Course's truth, nor that Jesus was the source of the material. In fact, she was always quite protective of the Course's purity, understanding it from deep within herself, and critical of those who distorted its teachings and sought to use *A Course in Miracles* for personal gain. She could always discern authenticity from inauthenticity and, to quote her favorite play *Hamlet*, knew "a hawk from a handsaw."

Rumors again to the contrary, Helen was never truly an atheist, although she did pose as one during the beginning of her professional career. Born Jewish, she had been a spiritual seeker since childhood with a special attraction to Roman Catholicism, though never subscribing to its doctrines or dogmas. Her love-hate relationship with the Church extended to Jesus, and she finally abandoned her spiritual quest in frustration and anger, believing that she had done her part in seeking God, but that He had not done His. Helen's struggles with Jesus, incidentally, can be seen in some of the poems she had taken down, published posthumously by the Foundation for Inner Peace as *The Gifts of God*. The full story of Helen's experiences in taking down the Course and her relationship with Jesus can be found in *Absence from Felicity: The Story of Helen Schucman and Her Scribing of A COURSE IN MIRACLES*, published by the Foundation for *A Course in Miracles*. Helen died in 1981, and Bill in 1988.

What *A Course in Miracles* Is

A Course in Miracles consists of three books—text, workbook for students, and manual for teachers—and is thus presented as a complete learning curriculum. It should be noted that it states that we are all teachers and students alike, so the three books are meant for all people who become students of the Course. The text provides the theoretical foundation for the practical application of its ideas found in the workbook, which consists of three hundred and sixty-five lessons, one for each day of the year. The third volume is the manual for teachers, and consists of questions and answers which summarize some of the more important themes found in the Course. An appendix to the manual includes a clarification of some of the Course's terms; this was taken down three years after the Course itself was completed.

A Course in Miracles makes no claim to being the only form of truth, nor the only spiritual path a person may choose back to God. In fact, it states that it is only one form "of the universal course... (among) many thousands of other forms, all with the same outcome" (manual, p. 3; M-1.4:1-2). Thus, despite sharing a common goal, all spiritualities can be seen to have certain unique aspects that distinguish them from each other. *A Course in Miracles* is not only unique but radical, in the etymological sense of going to the root of things. It repeatedly urges us to return to the root or original cause of our problems: the belief in our separation from God.

A Course in Miracles teaches that the way to remember the God Who created us is by undoing our guilt through forgiving others and therefore ourselves. Its focus is thus on the healing of relationships, which exist only within the mind (the source of the dream), though projected into the world (the dream) and experienced there. *A Course in Miracles* is unusual in its integration of a non-dualistic metaphysics with a practical psychology. In this regard, one of the most important statements the Course makes is that God, being a loving Creator, did not create this world. Far from leaving this idea as an abstract theological issue with no relevance to our daily lives, *A Course in Miracles* helps us recognize the extraordinary personal implications of this truth. In fact, one could say that without acceptance of this metaphysical premise, students would not be fully able to understand the Course's theoretical system, let alone apply its practical teachings on forgiveness to every area of their lives, without exception. Thus, the metaphysical statements on the nature of God and the world are integrated with a sophisticated psychology that help us to understand and apply its ontological teachings in order to achieve our individual salvation.

A *Course in Miracles* is also unique in its interesting blend of Eastern and Western thought. Its non-dualistic metaphysics has more parallels in the ancient teachings of Hinduism and Buddhism than in the dualistic thinking of the major Western religions. Yet the Course's language remains Judaeo-Christian, and the development of its theology, its principles of forgiveness, and the role of Jesus or the Holy Spirit occurs largely through their contrast with much of the biblical teachings.

INTRODUCTORY MATERIAL ON CHRISTIAN THEOLOGY

CATECHISM OF THE CATHOLIC CHURCH. Libreria Editrice Vaticana. MO: Liguori Publications, 1994.

FAITH SEEKING UNDERSTANDING: An Introduction to Christian Theology. Daniel L. Migliore. Grand Rapids, MI: William B. Eerdmann Publishing Co., 1991.

THE NEW TESTAMENT–AN INTRODUCTION: Proclamation and Parenthesis, Myth and History. Norman Perrin. NY: Harcourt, Brace, Jovanovich, 1982.

NEW TESTAMENT THEOLOGY. Joachim Jeremias. NY: Scribner's, 1971.

A SUMMARY OF CHRISTIAN FAITH: Catholic, Protestant, and Reformed. John H. Leith. Philadelphia: Westminster/John Knox Press.

RELATED MATERIAL ON *A COURSE IN MIRACLES*

By Kenneth Wapnick, Ph.D.

Books

CHRISTIAN PSYCHOLOGY IN *A COURSE IN MIRACLES*. Second edition, enlarged. Discussion of the basic principles of the Course in the context of some of the traditional teachings of Christianity. Includes a new Preface and an Afterword.
ISBN 0-933291-14-0 • #B-1• Paperback • 90 pages $4.

FORGIVENESS AND JESUS: The Meeting Place of *A Course in Miracles* and Christianity. Fourth edition. Discussion of the teachings of Christianity in the light of the principles of the Course, highlighting the similarities and differences; the application of these principles to issues such as injustice, anger, sickness, sexuality, and money.
ISBN 0-933291-13-2 • #B-5 • Paperback • 355 pages $16.

LOVE DOES NOT CONDEMN: The World, the Flesh, and the Devil According to Platonism, Christianity, Gnosticism, and *A Course in Miracles*. An in-depth exploration of the non-dualistic metaphysics of *A Course in Miracles*, and its integration with living in this illusory world.
ISBN 0-933291-07-8 • #B-9 • Hardcover • 614 pages $25.

ABSENCE FROM FELICITY: The Story of Helen Schucman and Her Scribing of *A Course in Miracles*. Discussion of Helen's lifetime conflict between her spiritual nature and her ego; includes some of her recollections, dreams, letters, and personal messages from Jesus—all never before in print; an account of her own experiences of Jesus, her relationship with William Thetford, and the scribing of the Course.
ISBN 0-933291-08-6 • #B-11 • Paperback • 521 pages $16.

Audio Tape Albums: Workshops and Classes

ATONEMENT WITHOUT SACRIFICE: Christianity, the Bible, and the Course. Workshop exploring the relationship between *A Course in Miracles* and the Judaeo-Christian tradition, with special emphasis placed on the role of sacrifice and suffering.
ISBN 0-933291-53-1 • #T-3 • 2 tapes $15.

JESUS AND *A COURSE IN MIRACLES*. Discussion of passages in the Course in which Jesus refers to himself: as the source of the Course; his historical teaching example as the manifestation of the Holy Spirit, and perfect model of forgiveness; and his role as our teacher, without whom the undoing of the ego's thought system would be impossible.
ISBN 0-933291-62-0 • #T-12 • 5 tapes $40.

JESUS AND THE MESSAGE OF EASTER. The Course's view of Jesus, and the meaning of his crucifixion and resurrection: our seeming sins against Jesus have had no effect, and so our seeming sin against God in the original instant of separation also had no effect.
ISBN 0-933291-71-X • #T-21 • 8 tapes $65.

THE METAPHYSICS OF SEPARATION AND FORGIVENESS. Summary of the teachings of *A Course in Miracles*, specifically showing how the principle that the thought of separation and the physical world are illusions becomes the foundation for the understanding and practice of forgiveness in our daily lives.
ISBN 0-933291-84-1 • #T-34 • 1 tape $6.

JESUS: THE MANIFESTATION OF THE HOLY SPIRIT. A discussion of Jesus and the Holy Spirit in the context of the difference between appearance and reality, and the importance of Jesus as our guide in leading us out of the dream; includes a discussion of the relationship of Jesus to Helen Schucman and to *A Course in Miracles*.
ISBN 0-933291-81-7 • #T-31 • 5 tapes $40.

FORGIVING JESUS: "Stranger on the Road." Discussion of our need to forgive Jesus because he is right and we are wrong about ourselves. The context is Helen Schucman's poem "Stranger on the Road," which expresses her experiences of the crucifixion and the resurrection, and reflects her conflicts—shared by practically all students of the Course—in developing a relationship with Jesus.
ISBN 0-933291-92-2 • #T-42 • 2 tapes $10.

THE BIBLE FROM THE PERSPECTIVE OF *A COURSE IN MIRACLES*. Kenneth and Gloria Wapnick. A presentation of the Bible and the Course as mutually exclusive spiritual paths, demonstrating that attempts to graft the Bible on to the Course result in the distortion and corruption of the meaning of both systems.The Course, with its non-dualistic God, and Jesus who teaches Atonement without sacrifice, is presented as the correction of the biblical thought system.
ISBN 0-933291-93-0 • #T-43 • 6 tapes $36.

THE THEOLOGY OF *A COURSE IN MIRACLES*. Kenneth and Gloria Wapnick. A presentation of the unique non-dualistic theology of *A Course in Miracles* contrasted with the dualistic theology of Judaism and traditional Christianity. The workshop focuses on the Course's radically different teachings on God, Jesus, sin, salvation, and Atonement, and the importance of these for the practice of forgiveness.
ISBN 0-933291-94-9 • #T-44 • 2 tapes $10.

Ordering Information

For orders *in the U.S. only*, please add $3.00 for the first item, and $1.50 for each additional item, for shipping and handling. Most orders are shipped UPS. However, orders to *P.O. Boxes, Alaska, Hawaii,* and *Puerto Rico* are shipped Parcel Post (add an additional $1.00 per item for First Class Mail).

New York State residents please add local sales tax. (New York law requires sales tax on shipping and handling charges.)

For *international orders*, please write or call the Foundation for *A Course in Miracles* (see below).

VISA and MasterCard accepted.

Order from:

Foundation for *A Course in Miracles*
1275 Tennanah Lake Road
Roscoe, NY 12776-5905
(607) 498-4116 • FAX (607) 498-5325

For a complete list of books and tapes, please call or write the
Foundation for *A Course in Miracles*.

* * * * *

A COURSE IN MIRACLES and other scribed material may be ordered from the Foundation for "A Course in Miracles," or from:

Foundation for Inner Peace
PO Box 598
Mill Valley, CA 94942
(415) 388-2060

A COURSE IN MIRACLES, Second edition:

> Three volumes: Hardcover $40
> One volume (complete): Hardcover: $30
> One volume (complete): Softcover: $25

PSYCHOTHERAPY: PURPOSE, PROCESS AND PRACTICE: $3.00
THE SONG OF PRAYER: PRAYER, FORGIVENESS, HEALING: $3.00
THE GIFTS OF GOD: $21.00

Additional copies of this book may be ordered from:

Foundation for *A Course in Miracles*
1275 Tennanah Lake Road
Roscoe, NY 12776-5905

Send a check or money order (in US funds only) for $5.00 plus
shipping: please see page 113 for shipping charges.